Alberta Galla

The most
Excursions
in Crete
Gorges Nature Archeology

MYSTIS
EDITIONS

Published by:

108 Menelaou Parlama St.. – Heraklion 75100– Crete
Tel. 2810 346451, Fax 2810 221908
Web site: www.mystis.gr E-mail: info@mystis.gr

Graphics and page layout: Giovanni Schettin
Illustrations by Cristina Cazzanello

Index

Introduction

This small guidebook contains twenty excursions that explore the island's most accessible and least known gorges. The excursions briefly touch portions of the E4 European long-distance hiking trail and also offer relaxing forays that are of botanical interest or lead to archeological sites that are only accessible on foot.

Each gorge has its own physiognomy, which unfolds as hikers make their way through it; each hike sparks a succession of sensations and rediscovered amazement in every season of the year. Gorges are joyous and boisterous in the springtime, when the courses of water insinuate themselves and widen out among the rocks; they are thirsty and arid in the summer, when they are inhabited by the sun and strong winds. They are peaceful in the fall, when they are barely animated by the muffled rustling of small rodents and the fluttering of partridges and pheasants; and mute and solemn in the winter, when they are often hard to penetrate. A gorge is a microcosm which, during the three or four hours it takes to hike through it, generates expectations of adventure and keeps its promise. The magic of its rocks alone makes it an "unicum;" terms like metamorphosis, loam rock or phyllite need to be decoded, but how can one help but be fascinated by the twinkling of mineral quartz, the severity of a volcanic shade of black, the liveliness of green serpentine, magnificent red shale, the wavy design and thin veins of sandstone!

During our excursions, we experience the three consecutive phases of fruition: in the beginning, the expectation, with preparations like choosing a destination and evaluating the difficult points in advance. Next comes the action, which generates enthusiasm because we are finally experiencing the hike. Lastly, the conclusion, the satisfaction of having completed the endeavor: the gorge has been conquered, the excursion is over.

Imbros Gorge

 Departure point: the village of Imbros
Destination: Komitades

 Hiking time: 2 hours one way

 Level of difficulty: easy

 Suitable for children

 Downhill trail with approx. 600 meters vertical drop

 Recommended time of the year: April to November

 Well-marked trail

 Carry along a normal supply of water

Imbros Gorge
The whims of the gorge.

Our first trekking experience was our exploration of the "farangi Imbrou" – the Imbros gorge. It was once the only pathway through the harsh, impassable mountains of the Sfakia region. This vital path allowed the area's inhabitants to remain in contact with the rest of the island in times of peace and to defend themselves by isolating themselves in times of war. We can well imagine how difficult it must have been to traverse this canyon, on foot or on muleback. Although the path starts out fairly easy, it soon increases in difficulty, disappearing and hiding among the rocks. Only at the end of the two-hour hike does the trail level out and become paved once again. Sfakia is a land of proud and courageous people, brusque-mannered inhabitants of few words. They might be impatient with tourism but at the same time they depend on it for their own survival. The many travelers who have ventured into this region over the centuries tell of tall, blond men with blue eyes. According to local folklore they might be the descendents of people who migrated from the north and have lived in isolation ever since, cut off by the natural barrier created by the mountains and ready to defend themselves from the sea. This land is made of sheer cliffs that loom over the shore and is furrowed by ravines of karst formations. It has many caves

but few forests and can only serve as pastureland. Today, meager stands of cypress trees and sessile oak survive exclusively in the gorges.

After the large village of Ammoudari, that spreads out like an amphitheatre in the green, fertile plain of Askifou and is safeguarded by an imposing Turkish fortress on the hilltop, the road narrows and begins to skirt the rocks, leveling out at the town of Imbros, the departure point of our

excursion. This village, located 700 meters above sea level, has many taverns that offer light meals, tempt visitors to purchase honey and local herbs, and supply information about the gorge. After leaving our car in the parking lot of one of these taverns we begin walking along a wide, downward-sloping path to the left of the main road, preceded by the cheerful voices of a group of excursionists wearing simple summer sandals. We're rather sorry that we can't enjoy the meditative silence offered by excursions undertaken in solitude, but we know that the shade and fresh air of the canyon are a valid enticement for so many hikers. After a hundred meters of easy descent, the real trail into the gorge begins, marked by a sign that announces "Imbros Gorge" and a stone construction that sells entrance tickets for two euros.

For the first half hour we follow a broad, monotonous path along the gray gravel of a dry riverbed, skirting large boulders and sparse vegetation composed of low, thorny bushes. Then the landscape slowly begins to change and turn woody, and the first majestic pine trees appear.

As we descend the path, the slopes of the gorge, which are made of yellowish-gray limestone streaked with broad, horizontal, black veins, rise up powerfully around us. The ravine is studded with small oak trees that

are amazingly rooted in the fissures of the rock face. It is October and this year Crete's endless summer has no intention of yielding to autumn, as it flaunts spiky lilac chastetrees, the purple flowers of mastic trees, umbrella-like tufts of spurge, and flowering oleanders. There are numerous natural caves along the rocky flanks of the gorge which once served as ideal hiding places for ambushes and offered refuge for women and children fleeing from enemy attacks, Venetian or Turkish alike.

After an hour we reach the heart of the canyon and our gaze rises awestruck to the pinnacles of red rock. From this point on we will be at the mercy of the whims of the gorge, which first magnanimously

offers us broad expanses dotted with maritime pines, plane trees and oak. Then suddenly the canyon turns malicious and creates obstacles, forcing us into obscure, narrow passages between its walls, from which we emerge into dazzling sunlight. It spitefully puts us to the ordeal of the "yoke" – in this case an enormous, horizontal tree trunk, whose naked roots are upturned to the sky and force us into contortions in order to get by. A bit further on is another astounding passage, a double tunnel of polished stone, a rocky "S" that is shiny and smooth. Only one person can pass at a time because it is only 1.60 meters at its widest. After overcoming this mini-labyrinth, there are more natural wonders to come: a daring example of Nature's architecture appears before us, a double, rocky arch ten meters high, the mighty ogive of a mineral cathedral.

This first hike of ours has taught us that the dramatic intensity of each gorge possesses a tangible supernaturalism. Their mystery seems to be easily accessible but, in fact, taking them on generates a realization of just how inadequate our human resources are.

Slowly but surely, the gorge begins to lose its ruggedness; it levels out among grassy verges, olive trees with vast trunks and fig trees laden with shriveled fruit. The path turns into an ancient mule track paved with large, regular stones, a prelude to our arrival in the town of Komitades. The savage enchantment is brusquely interrupted by a return to "civilization," a second checkpoint for tickets, followed by a kiosk selling drinks and snacks. We are offered the possibility of returning to our departure point by taxi. Our hike has lasted two hours,

we have walked six kilometers and are a bit tired. We let ourselves be tempted by the proposal. Our trip back to Imbros is highly singular; we are loaded into a pick-up truck whose cab is reserved for the women while the men sit in the uncomfortable, open-air truck bed. For those who decide to proceed by foot, the paved road continues for another half a kilometer to the town of Komitades, where we recommend an interesting side trip to the small church of Agios Georgios. The chapel is situated in the lower part of the village and can be reached by following a path for about one hundred meters that leads to it. Agios Georgios dates to the second Byzantine period; it is located on a rocky outcrop and over the centuries it has literally sunk into the earth. On the outside, traces of half bowls in the form of a cross adorn the façade, while inside it is decorated with frescos attributed to Giovanni Pagomeno, a 14th-century artist who was very active in the area.

Glikà Nerà - Loutrò

 Departure point: Chora Sfakion
Destination: Loutrò

 Hiking time: 2 hours

 Level of difficulty: fairly difficult

 Not suitable for children

 Trail without major variations in height

 Recommended time of the year: April to November

 Trail marked with trail signs and E4 signs

 Carry along a normal supply of water

Glikà Nerà - Loutrò

Sweet water, blue water!

Among the various hiking itineraries in this book, we have included a portion of the European long-distance hiking trail which is part of a project we have been nursing for some time: a two-day hike that includes a stop at Glikà Nerà beach, an overnight stay at Loutrò and an exploration of the Aradena gorge starting from enchanting Marmara beach. So many times, as we stood on the bridge of the ferry boat taking us to Paleochora we have contemplated this area, which holds a special allure for us because it is so difficult to reach by land. Each time the ferry docked for a few moments in this bay we regretted not having disembarked to enjoy the atmosphere.

Finally, one October afternoon, after an excursion to spectacular Imbros gorge, we reach Chora Sfakion and drive along the road leading to Anopoli. After roughly a kilometer and a half, we park our car in a clearing on a curve, put on our hiking boots and, backpack on shoulders, begin following the path indicated by a yellow and black sign marked E4. It takes two hours to hike four and a half kilometers. The path is difficult at times and sparks alternating emotions, slight trepidation over a few difficult passages, the joy of discovering Glikà Nerà, one of the most sensational beaches on this part of the island, and our arrival at Loutrò with an enchanted sunset.

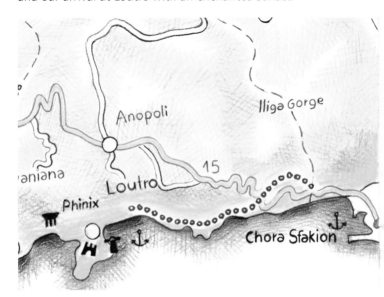

The crushed stone path leads alongside a sheer drop over the sea, among boulders that must be circumvented while carefully keeping one's back to the rock face. In a few points the high, rugged coastline offers breathtaking views of the sea and a palette of amazing colors. The cobalt blue of the deeper water near the jagged underwater caverns shades to turquoise blue and mixes with the emerald green of the sea glittering in the sun. After an hour's descent we arrive at Glikà Nerà, an extended silvery tongue of land protected by a massive, high wall of opalescent limestone. The beach's name refers to the "sweet water" of the natural springs that bubble up in various points along the sandy shore. These springs are wisely protected and marked by rings of large stones with rudimental stairs leading into the pools. Glikà Nerà is the destination of naturists, some of whom seem to be quite at home here, careful custodians who make sure that these springs remain uncontaminated. They firmly urge us to use the water from the containers that are already filled with the precious liquid and then to refill them for the next people. Two or three tamarisk trees and a few improvised tents made of large branches and colorful cloth offer the beach's only protection from the sun. At the western extremity of Glikà Nerà there is a small snack bar that rents deckchairs, as well as a dock for small boats (the last boat

for Loutrò leaves at five in the afternoon; the last boat for Chora leaves at 5:30 p.m.).

A few canoes are pulled up on the beach while others are slowly skimming their way ashore, a sign that some of the bathers are good rowers who have made their way here from nearby Chora or even from Loutrò.

There is a continuous coming and going of excursionists who, like us, couldn't resist the temptation of an afternoon swim in the cool water that is barely rippled by waves. After their swim, they wash off the sea salt with the sweet water from the springs.

It is getting late, we can't tarry any longer and thus begin walking along the mountain ridge to the west for ten minutes, passing by the small white church of Timios Stavros on a promontory known as Cape Punta before we begin to descend along a path that leads through a small forest of pine trees. We then head toward a heap of rocks and pass a tiny, isolated and rocky bay. The path leads upward

once again, a thin white line that parallels the mountain as it hugs the naked cliff face. The sun is about to set and is beginning to lose its vigor, thus giving us some respite from the heat. In the distance we can see the outline of Loutrò, white and blue, stretching along its natural bay that extends from the promontory of Moures to the southern, rocky offshoots of the White Mountain range.

We arrive at our destination, Loutrò, after a pleasurable hour's walk. We enter the town through a small gate and immediately have the feeling that we have entered a special world. The last rays of the sun tinge the smooth flanks of the mountain with red and are reflected off the white walls of the houses in the village. Loutrò's activity all takes place around the port, with rooms for rent, and taverns and small hotels in old stone buildings that have been restructured but maintain their traditional characteristics. From the terrace of our room the shadow of the promontory rapidly invades, swallows and

finally obscures the enormous rocky barrier that protects Loutrò to the east. As evening falls, a small ferryboat with a high-sounding name, the Daskaloghianni, docks in the port. A final clattering noise as the anchor is lowered into the sea and then we are enveloped in silence. The boat's white silhouette will motionlessly stand guard until the next morning.

The locals tell us that the name "Daskaloghianni" is in honor of a heroic event that occurred long ago, in 1769, when a small shipowner, Ioannis Vlachos, known as "Daskaloghianni" (Master John) tried to bring independence to the Sfakia region by leading the first rebellion against the Turks. The numeric superiority of the Turkish forces doomed the undertaking to failure and the epilogue was terrible. To avoid further bloodshed, Daskaloghianni spontaneously gave himself up to the Turkish authorities; he was taken to the fortress of Candia, (now known as Heraklion), tortured and flayed alive.

Aràdena Gorge

Departure point: Loutrò
Destination: Aràdena

Hiking time: 4 hours

Level of difficulty: challenging

Not suitable for children

Uphill trail with 700 meters vertical drop

Recommended time of the year: April to November

Trail with red markings that aren't always easily visible

Carry along an abundant supply of water

Aràdena Gorge
The climb

The ascension of the Aràdena gorge is the culmination of a two-day excursion during which we explored the E4 European long-distance hiking trail on the first day from Chora Sfakion to Loutro where we spent the night. We leave the village still immersed in the ecstatic torpor that pervades the coastline villages of Crete during the early hours of the morning. Out in the sleepy bay, which has yet to be touched by the first rays of the sun, someone is swimming tracing large circles in the lead-colored water. The ferryboat, the Daskaloghianni, which had anchored in the harbor the evening before, has disappeared. Leaving the port we take a pathway to the left that climbs upward toward the promontory of Moures, which has a small hilltop cemetery that dominates the sea and an archeological area with the remains of the ancient city of Phinix. We pass by the church of Christ the Savior (Christou Sotirou) with its 15th century frescos, and descend toward the cove of Finikas, the ancient port of Loutro, where the pathway leaves the coast and merges with the road leading to Livaniana, a small village clinging to the mountainside. Even though our map of the area is very detailed, we aren't sure we are going in the right direction. Only by following two foreigners

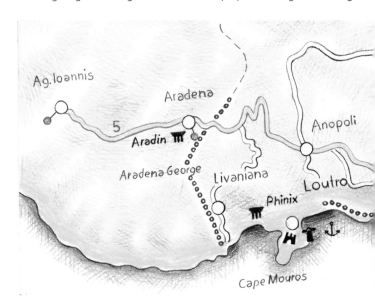

down a steep path to the sea do we reach Marmara bay, the departure point of our excursion. We are greeted by a small, white beach of fine pebbles which has several inviting grottos on the left that can be easily swum to in just a few strokes. The grottos slope gradually to the sea on slabs of marble with delicate opaline veining. There is a café on a rocky outcropping above the cove that serves food. Close by, several simple, white cubes of cement are scattered around on the bare earth, Spartan bungalows ready to host visitors who seek solitude and absolute sea.

After enjoying the traditional reward of people who have descended the gorge - a swim in the superb emerald water - we prepare to explore, equipped with hiking boots, snacks and lots of drinking water. Mount Kefala, solemn and impassible with its deep vertical gash, rises before us. This is a magical moment because we are about to fulfill a long-standing wish: to hike through the compact, pearly canyon that connects Marmara with the ancient village of Aràdena.

The trail forcefully makes its way into the canyon between two narrow vertical walls which offer some respite from the burning,

late-autumn sun only in the early stages of our hike. The path leads along a dry riverbed as it winds its way between large boulders, stops in front of the most cumbersome and then widens out into a clearing of crushed stone below the craggy peaks. Along our way, we are struck by the majesty of the pines - pinus Brutia or Alepensis. Imperious and solitary, they flank the pathway and then cluster together in large numbers where the sides of the gorge widen out, shading the ground with their verdant branches.

During the first hour of the hike, the pathway is not well marked. We know that there are seven challenging points during the five and a half kilometers to come, rocky obstacles that must be climbed bare-handed, and we willingly take on the challenge. We meticulously search for the red-painted trail markers but the double markings in the first part of the hike throw us off course, leading us in the wrong direction and up a steep and dangerous ridge. After arriving at the rocky hilltop, the broader view shows us that our true path

was close by, along a riverbed invaded by numerous tufts of tall grass. The simplest rule in these situations is, perhaps, to also trust in the rudimental markers made of small pyramids of stones that excursionists always leave behind as proof of their passage and to reassure those who follow that they are on the right path.. We stop frequently to rest along the tiring and impervious trail, to restore our energy with food and water, and to enjoy the majestic setting dominated by the towering red rocks. We are surrounded by a potpourri of fragrant herbs like thyme, winter savory, lavender and wild oregano. The 700 meters of vertical drop of the trail leading from the sea to Aràdena are often invaded by oleander bushes and chastetree shrubs, and strong oak trees are infallible sentinels marking underground sources of water. After roughly two hours of hiking, the path forks and two gaudy blue arrows indicate two alternative itineraries: to the right, Livaniana, and to the left, Aghios Ioanni. We ignore both arrows and continue on straight ahead. After ten minutes the path widens out to a large clearing, the last picnic area in the shade of the towering walls, where a merry, noisy group of French people are eating. This was once the crucial point of the excursion because there was only one way to continue, by climbing an enormous boulder with only the help of a simple rope. This rudimental solution was later substituted by an iron ladder about ten meters tall. Nonplussed, we abandon our original project of attempting this famous ladder because it looks too difficult and unsteady. We opt for a third alternative that was recently created: a pathway dug into the rock face and equipped with a tortuous, wooden guardrail that follows along the mountain ridge and looks out over the void.

After carefully completing this portion of the trail, in the distance

we can hear a strange noise that is amplified by the rocky mountain sides, a rattling sound we can't identify at first. The mystery is re solved a hundred meters further on, when we raise our eyes and se above us the powerful pylons of an iron Bailey bridge. The deafening metallic noise is caused by the infrequent cars crossing the bridge We feel dwarfed by this gigantic viaduct, which we must somehov reach. The sides of the canyon that the bridge spans are scored b two wide, paved paths that zigzag up the gorge, creating a specta cular stone embroidery on the red mountainside. For centuries loca inhabitants have crossed these two tracks on foot or on muleback for these paths were once the only connection between Anopo

and the villages of Aràdena and Aghios Ioannis. Then in 1986, a wealthy Athenian fa mily, that was originally from Aghios Ioannis, had the daring bridge built.

We walk along the mule path on the left side of the mountain, dragging oursel ves in exhaustion for the las twenty minutes, until we re ach the first abandoned hou ses of Aràdena. Constructed on the site of the ancien city-state of Aradin, this town is an interesting example o Crete's traditional architectu re, a ghost village that houses an extraordinary gem, the church dedicated to Saint Michael the Archangel. The church, which was built on the ruins of a Paleo-Christian basilica, is in the form of a Byzantine cross and inside has precious frescos dating back to the fourteenth century.

After crossing the Bailey bridge and admiring the fearsome void below, we feel proud of our accomplishment and finally catch our breath, sitting on the edge of the road and enjoying the view of the peaks of the Lefka Ori range, clear and white-capped, with their dark hem of pine forests. It took us four hours to ascend, counting the hour-long hike between Loutro and Marmara, which lazier excursionists can avoid by taking a boat that leaves every day from Loutro at 11 a.m. or by hiring a boat for a small sum.

We hitch-hike in hopes of a lift back to Chora Sfakion, thirteen kilometers away. It takes quite a while before a charitable Greek tourist, intrigued by our mountain gear and curious to learn about our unusual experience, agrees to accompany us back to our starting point.

Agia Irini Gorge

Departure point: Agia Irini
Destination: Snack bar Oasi - end of the gorge
(two-hour hike to Sougia)

Hiking time: 3 hours downhill

Level of difficulty: easy

Suitable for children

Downhill trail with 400 meters vertical drop

Recommended time of year: April to November

Path with trail markers

Drinking water available along the trail

Agia Irini Gorge
The enchanted forest

Not as well known and certainly less difficult than the nearby gorge of Samaria, Agia Irini gorge has its own intrinsic beauty, made of sweeping views, the possibility of hiking in solitude and a relatively easy path without any difficult points to overcome. To reach it, we leave Chania and follow the highway that crosses the island from north to south all the way to Sougia. We drive through citrus fruit orchards and head in the direction of Omalos, toward the northernmost edge of the White Mountains. At Alikianos we make a detour to drive through valleys of chestnut trees, whose spiky, dark brown fruit thickly carpets the ground all the way to the edge of the roadside. We pass by abandoned villages, Papadiana, Nea Roumata, Prasses, Agia Irini, and after passing this last village, a sign on the left and a map of the trail indicate the entrance to the gorge. After paying the symbolic entrance fee of one euro, we immediately find ourselves in a dark, wild forest, a mountain tangle of majestic pine trees, enormous plane trees and leafy oaks lining a riverbed. We cross a small, slightly shaky bridge made of wooden planks and start down the trail. The first portion leads upward, with the deep chasm on the right and a sturdy wooden fence protecting the trail in the more difficult points. After overcoming the trickiest part of the ravine, the trail begins its descent along wide curves all the way to a first picnic area,

which has a fountain.

The sun warms us and at the same time it protects us from a wind that is so strong that we think we hear the rushing sound of water down in the valley. We soon realize it is actually the sound of rustling oak leaves, infinitely amplified. The atmosphere is so magical that we wouldn't be surprised to encounter "Pizia" – the ancient priestess whose oracles were inspired by the rustling sound of the leaves - sitting underneath one of these trees. After walking for an hour, we are surrounded by the penetrating perfume of wild sage, for a thick tract of these aromatic bushes covers an entire slope. It is Crete's "faskomilo," also known as salvia fruticosa, with its characteristic light green leaves covered with a whitish fuzz. There is so much

sage that a young Greek excursionist behind us marvels that he can smell the scent of tea. This observation isn't as odd as it might seem because, in Crete, these labiates are used in infusions. "Vounatiko Tchai," mountain tea, is a very popular drink that is sweetened with honey and warms the inhabitants up on the rare cold winter day in Crete; it is also considered a failsafe antidote against colds. We continue to descend the gorge along a zigzag path for another hour, from one hairpin turn to the next, all the way to the bottom. The pine trees gradually diminish, making way for small oak trees and majestic plane trees. We come upon the huge trunk of one of these trees, over fifteen meters long, lying alongside the trail. The underbrush has ferns and mushrooms very similar to porcini; most likely

they are Boletus appendicularis, a type of mushroom that goes very well with meat dishes. Bluish on the inside, their preferred habitat is any broad-leafed tree, in particular oak. A solemn silence envelops us, we feel tiny and lost at the bottom of the valley and, like in other gorges, we are struck by the absence of birdsong. One last stop in a vast picnic area – we have counted three along the way – with a natural spring gurgling from the rocks. The gorge gradually widens and flattens out, leaving behind the rocky peaks and making its way among chastetree and oleander bushes. The landscape is softer now, almost domesticated, with olive trees planted in orderly rows. A wooden arrow, with the Greek word "exodos" indicates the exit and a few meters farther on a pleasant tavern-snack bar appears. It is very similar to an Alpine chalet-refuge and is still open even though we are well into October. The hike has lasted three hours, with a 400 meter vertical drop from start to finish. Now we must find a way

to reach the nearest town, Sougia; we call a taxi, whose number is listed in the parking lot of the tavern. The alternative is a rather monotonous, two-hour hike along the paved road.

We were last in Sougia a couple of years ago and nothing seems to have changed, it is as tranquil as ever. Rooms for rent and small pensions, taverns and a few bars are lined up along the seashore. The beach is very nice, with fine gray sand and pebbles. It is protected to the east by the foot of Mount Chondrous Volakous; a few reefs in the sea animate the surface of the water. The atmosphere here is rather special and visitors might feel like they have been transported

in time back to the 1970s because there are many elderly hippies around with white beards and a foreign look about them. These bizarre characters stroll around naked and undisturbed along the water's edge; they swim in the sea or putter around their old campers, which don't seem to have ever been moved, as witnessed by the laundry hanging between one tamarisk tree and another and the "household" objects scattered about.

LISSOS

 Departure point: Sougia
Destination: Lissos- Bay of Agios Kyrkos

 Trekking time: 3 hours round trip

 Level of difficulty: easy

 Suitable for children

 Uphill and downhill trail with 200 meters vertical drop

 Recommended time of the year: March to December

 Well-marked trail

 Carry along a normal supply of water

LISSOS

A pilgrimage to the beneficial source

Our last excursion was to Agia Irini gorge and we spent the night at Sougia. Early the next morning, after a hearty breakfast we head to the small port for a short hike, three and a half kilometers on the European trail that in an hour and a half leads to the ancient city of Lissos. The day is clear; the strong wind has swept away the clouds overnight. People are already swimming in the sea while the locals enjoy their first coffee and regulation cigarette of the morning. Today is a special day for Greeks because it celebrates "No" day, a civil anniversary of Greece's refusal to let Mussolini and his troops cross through Greek territory. This day, October 28th, also marks the end of the tourist season and the day the people of Crete regain possession of their island. The kafeneion are once again full during the day and the evenings revolve around the "kazani," the stills for the home-made distillation of the local grappa known as "raki "o "tsikoudia."

No boats move in the bay. The lower portion of the white cliff has an odd horizontal stripe of black rock which, according to geologists, indicates the high-water mark when the sea rose seven meters 2,500 years ago. A sign with an arrow indicates Lissos and we start

down the trail that leads into a small ravine with lots of rock roses and pine, cypress and carob trees. The path leads gently upward, with many strokes of red paint indicating the way. We frequently stop to listen to the rustling of the forest, as the wind lightly blows through the branches. After half an hour, an impressive, concave rocky wall with wide, vertical ochre bands interrupts our tranquil hike. Menacing and impenetrable, it obliges us to clamber up the left side of the hill, which is covered with maritime pines. Even though the altitude we reach is modest, it nevertheless offers a generous view of the east side of the beach of Sougia, nestled among the green mountains of the district of Selino. The narrow trail transforms itself into a broad, ancient path paved with large stones. This path

has been trodden throughout the centuries, not by one-day excursionists with backpacks and alpenstocks, but by long processions of pilgrims - men, women, children, elderly people on muleback, provisions – heading for the beneficial water of the spring near the temple of Asclepius to cure their bodies with the precious liquid and appease their souls with votive offerings to the divinity. But it only takes us modern wanderers a quarter of an hour to reach the vast plain located 150 meters above sea level. The plain is protected to the north by the round forms of the Pelekania mountains, schistose and limestone formations that can be easily crossed from north to south, and has many abundant springs and forests of chestnut trees.

We are well into autumn now and we don't expect to find any flowers on the sunny plateau, a broad heath with dry bushes of spiny euphorbia, thyme, rock roses and a few solitary pines. But the beautiful lilac colchicums that cover the path are a surprise and we also come upon sweet pink cyclamens protected by brambles, an

unexpected gift. We head toward the southern end of the moor and begin our descent down wide, rocky, hairpin curves, distracted by the abundance of cyclamens that invade the path, emerge from the rocks or peep out from the twisted roots of pine trees. This variety cyclamen graecum, which in olden times was called "chelonian" – turtle – because of the similarity between the tubers and a turtle's shell, is a delicate shade of pink, with chordate leaves marked with gray-green veining. From here we can see our destination, the bay of Agios Kyrkos and the vast archeological area of Lissos. It takes twenty minutes to follow the broken path down along the slope among boulders and small stands of carob trees, until we reach a level area with the most important ruins of this city-state, which was once part of the mountain League of the Oreii. Lissos already existed in the third century B.C. and flourished until the Saracen invasion in the ninth century A.D.

The archeological site is unguarded; we easily cross the wire fencing that is broken in several places and enter the area of the temple dedicated to Asclepius, the Greek god of medicine and healing. Before entering the atrium of the temple, a series of steps lead to the thermal spring, whose water still wells forth. The building is a small Hellenistic construction of the Doric order, dating from the 4th to the 3rd century B.C. Low stone seating runs around the interior of the building and a Roman mosaic pavement from the first century A.D occupies much of the floorspace. A geometric symphony in black and white mosaic tesserae is set inside a beautiful spiral frame with different types of decorative panels. Without a doubt the most interesting panel is the central one: a thin labyrinth of lines with natu-

alistic drawings, a quail on a blue background, its tesserae feathers shading from beige to brown. On the western side, near the alter, there is a hollow that was probably meant for the sacred serpent, the symbol of medical science and a mandatory presence in every sanctuary since it was believed that snakes had healing powers.

Fragments of twenty statues have been found here, as well as marble ornaments from a sacred road and a headless statue of Asclepius, that is now at the archeological museum of Chania. Near the temple is the church of Agios Kyrkos, that was built on the ruins of a basilica, with interesting frescos inside and more mosaics in the courtyard in front of the church.

To the west, on the hillside, there is an impressive necropolis of vaulted tombs, a burial ground that is perhaps of Cilician origin, similar to ruins excavated by archeologists in nearby Sougia. Now the trail widens out on a vast plain and leads in different directions. The

European hiking trail continues to the west, crossing the hill and leading to Paleochor. To the east, the trail winds its way through a true archeological park with Corinthian capitals and columns lying on the ground, taking hikers to a small beach of white pebbles. The bright sunlight and the breeze animate the surface of the sea with countless sparkles of light. Despite the fairly brisk temperature we indulge ourselves in a dip in the sea, swimming out to the high ca-

vernous wall of the bay. A boat appears from behind the promontory, from the direction of Sougia; it lands and a couple with a child disembark. Without a doubt this is the boat of "Capitan George," who has obsessively advertised himself with posters all along our excursion, as though to reassure tired hikers that they can quickly return to Sougia by sea.

A few meters inland from the shore, slightly to the side, there is the chapel of Panagia – the Virgin – embedded in the ground. Its façade of naked stone is embellished with insertions that are clearly of Roman origin, pieces of entablature and a fragment of a sarcophagus from Asia Minor with the head of a Medusa. The osmosis between Roman Hellenistic paganism and Christianity is complete.

We start back the way we came, accompanied by bright sunlight and a brisk breeze. Our pilgrimage only lasted an afternoon, but we

are well satisfied with this happy combination of hiking, sea and archeology.

Anidri Gorge

Departure point: Anidri
Destination: the beach of Gialiskari

Hiking time: two and a half hours – 1 hour
to descend, one and a half hours to return

Level of difficulty: easy

Suitable for children

Trail with approx. 200 meters vertical drop

Recommended time of the year: April to November

Well-marked trail with trail signs

Carry along a normal supply of water

Anidri Gorge
Among the rock gardens

Selino and environs enjoy a happy dichotomy of nature and ar
The area's morphological characteristics - low, uncrowded, rounde
mountains, valleys of chestnut groves and strawberry trees studde
with bright red fruit – blend with ancient villages full of frescoe
churches and chapels, the most authentic expression of sacred ar
produced by Crete's artists from the year 1000 to the first half c
the 15th century. This distinctiveness, combined with an extensiv
coastline on the Libyan Sea with large and small bays of rare beaut
stretching from Sougia all the way to Elafonissi, make Selino an idea
location in our search for "eclectic" excursions that offer not jus
fascinating natural settings but cultural and spiritual stimulation a
well.

Our exploration of Anidri and its small, homonymous gorge is
perfect example of our goal. The "high points" of the excursion are
visit to the frescoed chapel of Aghios Georgios (St. George) in Anidr
at the beginning; our foray into the gorge as the naturalistic inter
mezzo; and our destination, an enchanting cove, at the end.

To reach Anidri, we drive along the eastern shore of Paleochora
with its numerous cafés and taverns, heading in the direction of th

campsite. Then, for roughly 6 kilometers we follow a winding road that crosses a narrow, shady valley. Anidri is nestled among the foothills of Mount Papoura; it faces a leafy gorge and catches a glimpse of the sea in the distance. The village has an air of antiquity, with ow, whitewashed houses and vegetable patches crowding the street with the fall's harvest of large, yellow squash, flask-shaped with ong, narrow necks. In the small, central square, the old elementary school has been transformed into a nice snack bar called "To Skoleio - The school house." The snack bar is run by pleasant German women who sell delicious homemade cakes and tempting sandwiches.

This is where our excursion begins, with three indications written in English: "to the church," "to the gorge," "to the beach" – three successive destinations that we fully explore in just over an hour.

The church of Aghios Georgios is located in the village's small cemetery, where a great many of the tombs all have the same last name. The church has two naves, is surmounted by a capital with the engraved bell in the center, and is completely frescoed inside. The most precious paintings are located in the north-western nave; they date back to 1323 and were painted by the 14th century artist Giovanni Pagomeno. His work is characterized by large, expressive faces, the freedom and airiness of his lines and the disguised realism in his rendering of the saints' solemnity. We imagine that he was called here by the small group of people who commissioned the work and who are named in the epigraph. The priest Nestore, the monk Isaia Mamos and the noble families of the area - Papadopouli, Meropouli, Skordili - must have paid Pagomeno in silver "iperperi," the money used at the time, which the artist spent on room and board, as well as on the powders and herbs he needed to mix his colors like the carmine red of the patron saint's cuirass and the ochre of the Virgin's halo.

After this plunge into Medieval religious art we are spiritually prepared for our hike. Near the chapel of Saint George, a sign announcing "beach" is perched in the hollow of an olive tree and sets us off along a paved road among contorted, knotty olive trees whose skinny branches reach to the sky like the arms of a thousand-year-old Methuselah. We pass cultivated fields and two lovely houses owned by Germans, as is indicated on the front gate. A stone stairway, which perhaps used to lead to the old wash-house conducts us down to the bed of a stream, the Dichalomata, which

at the moment is dry. But the vegetation that surrounds us with the perfume of spiky myrtle, the dark carob trees, tenacious chaste trees, and still flowering oleanders all indicate that in the wintertime the dry stream becomes a copious torrent. We walk along an easy path that is flanked by the black, snake-like tubes of the waterworks that accompany us to the end of the ravine. In the first part of our hike the low sides of the gorge are reassuring, we aren't compressed between towering, rocky walls. In fact, we don't even need to follow the usual path markers created by the little pyramids of stones. But these markers have extraordinary artistic value because the imagination of one or more improvised naturalistic artists has created extravagant rock gardens, minimalist sculptures of stones and contorted pieces of wood that enliven an otherwise rather monotonous hike. As we advance, the sides of Anidri gorge begin to rise more steeply and further on our progress is hampered by cumbersome piles of boulders that have fallen from the peaks above us over time and then been dragged downstream by the force of the water.

The gulch provides the one thrill of the entire excursion. After thirty-five minutes, a passage forces us to slide down a long smooth hollow for a few meters and land with the help of a robust rope that is well-anchored to the rock. Toward the end of the hike, the walls of Mount Papoura tower above us with their luxuriant maquis, and we enjoy the refreshment of a cool drink of water in a picnic area. Along the wall to the left of us there are reddish grottos of various dimensions, one in particular, that is over three meters high, reminds us that Crete has over three thousand caverns which have always been used as places of worship and refuge.

The deafening sound of angry waves warns us that we are near the sea. A faded sign advertises beauty treatments on the beach using the term that is so popular nowadays, "spa!" The two sandy shores of Gialiskari are nearby, divided by a low stand of Phoenician Juniper. The sea is choppy, we don't dare go for a swim and instead rest on the fine sand made of crushed rock. We are the only ones around; faint tracks on the sand and the solitary markers of the European trail seem to invite us to head east and cross the flanks of the promontory of Cape Flomes to discover another gem of the island, the Hellenistic and Roman archeological site of Lissos.

We retrace our steps back up the gorge and as we approach our starting point we notice signs of construction which could one day threaten this small Eden and cancel its savage beauty forever. It took us over two hours to complete the descent and return.

From Cape Krios to Elafonìssi

Departure point: Cape Krios
Destination: Elafonissi

Hiking time: 5 hours

Level of difficulty: fairly difficult

Not suitable for children

Trail without an excessive vertical drop

Recommended time of the year: March to December

Trail with markers and E4 signs

Carry along an abundant supply of water

From Cape Krios to Elafonìssi

To the cedar forest

This portion of the European long-distance trail, from Cape Krios to Elafonìssi, is a fairly long excursion, roughly five hours, and it could ideally be divided into three parts thanks to the variety of landscapes that it offers. The first part begins in the maquis of the promontory of Krios, stretches out along the shore with exceptional views of the sea, and ends one and a half hours later at the small church of Agios Ioannis. The second part, which is longer and more monotonous, leads from the church along a dry riverbed, crosses the rocky flanks of the coast along a trail halfway up the mountain and takes roughly one and a half hours. The third segment, which is the loveliest, leads to the bay of Vroulias and ends in glory at Elafonìssi, a two-hour hike in part along the seaside among sandy dunes and in part through a forest of cedars.

We start off in Paleochora, a small seaside town with the ruins of an ancient fortress on a hilltop. Eight kilometers later we reach the protected, sandy beach of Cape Krios, the last offshoot of the south-western coast. We park our car at the edge of a small forest of maritime juniper and walk along the deserted beach that is divided in two by a smooth boulder with the first signpost featuring the yellow and black logo of the E4 European trail. It is early November, the Libyan Sea is rather choppy, fast-moving clouds continuously block the sun. Our hiking boots sink into the light gray stones of the beach until a bright blue arrow invites us up a path along a short gully,

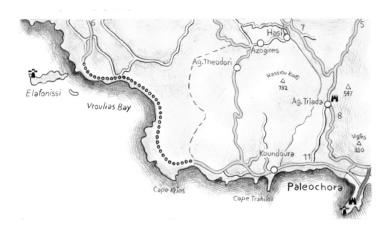

among rock rose bushes, low, cuspidate shrubs of Phoenician juniper and the umbrella-shaped flowers of dendroid Euphorbia. We quickly reach the saddleback of the promontory; in the distance we can see the silhouette of Elafonissi (Deer Island), hidden in a pale blue haze. Now the trail merges with a broad, white track that is occupied by a flock of sheep which indifferently ignore our presence. Fifteen minutes later we have left the earthen road behind and diligently follow the blue signs as we climb up a hillside and the maquis is gradually substituted by gariga, irregular vegetation that alternates with open areas and rocky outcroppings. The trail has frequent red markings and after crossing a gully full of Phoenician juniper we begin to

descend, making our way through a labyrinth of sharp pinnacles toward the promontory's first bay, which is dotted with myriads of dark concretions emerging from the surface of the water. The water's edge, which is occupied by a troop of black goats obstinately searching for tufts of grass, also features large, inanimate marble cylinders that have been devoured by the salt air, the ruins of columns with light green and pink veining. We are perplexed because although our map indicates an archeological site, the Hellenistic-Roman basilica of Viennos, no signs confirm its presence. We decide against going for a swim in the sea because the hike will be a long

one and we make do with dipping our fingers into the tepid water as though it were a holy water font. The trail leads upward once again, with a view of the sharp rocks below. One of these rocks has a blue and white votive edifice on it, an act of propitiation to the gods of the sea or a compassionate gesture in memory of a sad event?

After crossing another small forest of Phoenician junipers with their dark red, cone-shaped fruit, we carefully round the mountainside, one step at a time, well aware that we are dangerously exposed to the overhanging cliff. A few difficult meters and the trail becomes safe once again. We near our first destination, that is heralded by

a clearing of pink oleanders. In a leafy hollow we see the white silhouette of the church of Agios Ioannis. The chapel was constructed on a low slope, its whitewashed façade looks very old, with a hint of small, carved columns and a Gothic ogive lunette decorating the small entrance door. Agios Ioannis is locked; we vainly search for the key in the fissures of the architrave and then peer through the small window of the apse to get a glimpse of the interior of the chapel. In the shade of a carob tree in the little courtyard in front of the church, we enjoy the fantastic panorama below us of the wide expanse of bright green that ends in the pinkish sand of a cove with turquoise water.

We are ready to take on the second portion of the hike, another hour and a half along the crest of the mountain. We avoid the impassible rocky stretches of the coast until the red trail markings take us along a sandy, semicircular hollow to a long tongue of land, rocky

and white, that runs parallel to the sea. We soon regain altitude, following a precarious pathway that leads among the boulders of the disturbing mountain rifts above us. The trail is softened by sporadic bushes of pink heather with small, bell-shaped flowers. The trail markers are everywhere and very welcome. An E4 sign hangs despondently from the blackened branches of a leafless carob tree; we fear that furious thunderstorms are a regular occurrence in this area. We are surrounded by a landscape of arid frigana, a further degradation of the gariga, and round bushes that are thorny and aromatic. The use of these two terms, gariga and frigana, isn't meant to flaunt difficult words but rather, we believe, is a helpful way to gain more specific knowledge of the natural characteristics of the island.

The third phase of the excursion begins when we sight another small oasis of oleanders growing along a dry riverbed with large, marble-veined limestone outcroppings. Nature has been generous in this mini-canyon, offering small, wild olive trees, fragrant sage, myrtle shrubs and bushes of ballotta acetabulosa with their round, fuzzy leaves. The descent ends at the small beach of a lagoon located just before the gulf of Vroulias. From this point on we will be active spectators of a show of extraordinary beauty, a long series of rocky coves which an imaginative mind has drawn in the most diverse forms, the coriaceous tail of a prehistoric animal, the curved claws of a gigantic shrimp, a titanic hook. As seductive as sirens, these coves invite us into their bright wavelets. Bewitched, we advance slowly over the fine sand, uncertain as to which cove to elect as our ideal stop. Our perseverance is soon rewarded, the archetype of the ideal bay appears alongside a magnificent forest of cedar trees that almost touch the sea. A place like this could easily

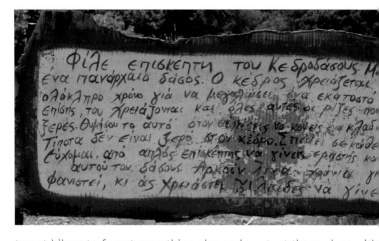

tempt hikers to forget everything else and content themselves with so much beauty, to stop and not continue further on. We have been hiking for four hours now and are beginning to feel tired. The clouds, which had scattered a few drops of rain at the beginning of the excursion, have been dissolved by a strong sun, all the more reason to abandon ourselves to a restorative swim. The first few meters of the transparent water reveal white slabs of underwater rock, a regal, mother-of-pearl coating that welcomes us in the fresh water that enchants and invigorates. Refreshed, we emerge from the water and seek shade under a cedar tree. Our attention is captured by the unusual morphology of this tree, whose trunk is grooved by thin vertical filaments and whose woody roots, even though they emerge from the ground and are suspended in the air, are nonetheless alive because they are nourished by the earth below. It is a prickly juniper tree - juniperus oxycedrus maxicarpa; this tree prefers steep shores and sandy beaches and is protected by the European Community. In Crete it can only be found here and on the small islands of Chrissi and Gavdos.

Among the dunes interspersed with pungent, horizontal tufts of ammophila arenaria, there are two sun-loving nudists, a few tents and an inviting hammock suspended between two large cedar branches. At the edge of the forest a hand-written sign informs passersby that cedar trees are very delicate; they can be damaged by any kind of encroachment and their roots take one hundred years to grow. The sign ends with a heartfelt entreaty to respect this protected species.

A few more kilometers to Elafonìssi; we slowly continue on as we savor the views of this stupendous landscape. Other trail markers appear among the black rocks near the sea but it is wiser to continue along the path marked by the tiny pyramids of stones. We come upon a sign announcing when the boat between Elafonìssi and Paleochora passes in high season; a man and a woman are intently fishing with long fishing poles. After another hour we sight a group of run-down campers, an unsightly summer campsite that is now abandoned and guides us to the famous beach.

Early on we had exchanged information with a group of vigorous, middle-aged German women but since then we have almost always been on our own. Our destination, Deer Island, can be reached by wading through a stretch of lagoon whose water occasionally reaches hip-deep. A sign lists the rules for enjoying this subtropical paradise in full respect of its fragile habitat. On a sandy hillside we admire two late flowerings of sea daffodils - pancratium maritimum; white and slender, these flowers bloom at the end of August. With its small, solitary coves, Elafonissi is enchanting at this time of year. The summer amusement park with its music, refreshment stands, beach umbrellas and paddleboats that spring up on the vast beach in front of us has disappeared with the first autumn rainfalls and we enjoy the beauty in total silence until sunset.

Katholikò Gorge

 Departure point: the convent of Gouverneto
Destination: the sea – end of the gorge

 Hiking time: 2 ½ hours round trip

 Level of difficulty: fairly difficult

 Not suitable for children

 Downhill trail with approx. 200 meters vertical drop to the sea

 Recommended time of the year: April to November

 Well-marked trail

 Carry along a normal supply of water

Katholikò Gorge
"Sublime" hiking

This hike, which led us to discover the convent of Saint John the Hermit (Xeno), known as "Katholikò," and the gorge of "the Saint," is a tangible example of the concept of the sublime as applied to places that can spark strong emotions. In this case, the romantic ruins of an ancient monastery suspended over a cliff and the formidable view of the canyon which leads to the sea. The beginning of this new excursion also offers a highly valid side trip because to reach our departure point we must cross the promontory of Akrotiri, north of Chania. There are three monasteries worth visiting along the way: the 16th century Saint John Eleimon (the Charitable), the architectural pearl Agia Triada Zangarol and austere Gouverneto. Driving down the road that leads to the airport we first come upon the small convent-fortress of Saint John Eleimon, which has been beautifully restored and conserved, leaving the pinkish rocks of the external wall visible. The ochre silhouette of Agia Triada Zangarol can be seen in the distance to the north. An avenue five kilometers long and lined with cypress and pine trees leads to this imposing monastery complex, a masterpiece of Renaissance architecture. We admire the elegance of its façade and the stairway framing a sumptuous entrance with double Corinthian columns topped by a tympanum. Peak tourist season is

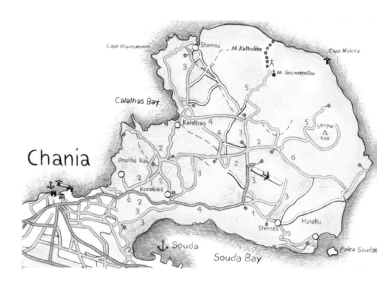

 over, we enter the empty courtyard dominated by the Renaissance church at its center. Arches and porticos with the monks' cells line the perimeter of the courtyard.

We leave Agia Triada immersed in its early-morning splendor; on our right we pass some stone farm buildings in which autumn agricultural activity is in a ferment and continue along a narrow road that climbs among rocky hillsides dotted with carob trees and thorny bushes. We cross a small gully invaded by goats and their cute kids and two kilometers later we reach the saddleback where Gouverneto is located. This rectangular monastery-fortress has square towers defending its corners and, although less elegant than the preceding monastery, it has its own rugged allure, with its parched earth, bleak hillsides and horizontal seascape in the distance. We leave our car in the large parking lot in front of the convent and begin our excursion in silence along an irregularly paved road. A vigorous sun and light breeze are our companions as we walk among spiny spurge, asphodels and large bulbs of common Dragon arum - dracunculus vulgaris schott, a plant with black markings on its stem that flowers in the springtime with amazing purplish bracts. Fifteen minutes later we make our first stop, a visit to the small rocky church of the Madonna

of the Bear (Panagia Arkoudiotissa), nestled at the opening of a tall, broad, circular grotto.

The chapel's entrance is divided into two rooms; the central room has an enormous stalagmite that recalls the shape of a bear. Legend has it that this vast karstic grotto was the home of a ferocious beast that used to drink the water from a well in front of the chapel, thus depriving the monks of the precious fluid. One day the monks decided to lay in wait for the bear; suddenly its large silhouette invaded the entire grotto, blocking the light completely. The frightened monks began to pray to the Virgin Mary, invoking her help, and the power of their prayers turned the bear into stone. But local tradition also has a basis of truth because the surrounding mountains are called Arcoudovouna – the mountains of the bear - and archeologists have found artifacts in this area pertaining to the worship of Artemis, the goddess of the hunt, which have to do with the figure of a bear, an animal that was sacred to her.

The trail becomes steeper and proceeds along tight turns. In front of us the view opens out toward the final offshoots of the promontory, while to the east it reveals the sides of a narrow gorge leading down to the sea. After twenty minutes the path comes to an end and turns into a long series of 120 wide steps. It passes the grotto with the venerated tomb of the convent's founder, John Xeno, and leads to the monastery of Katholikò, which is precariously perched over a gully. We are greeted by a lovely portal with capitals leading into a small courtyard in front of the rocky church, which has a beautiful bell tower supported by an ogive arch. The monastery dates back to 900 A.D. and daringly straddles the two sides of the gorge, which are connected by a wide, single-span bridge that creates a vast embankment where the buildings for the prior and the monks were located. The monastery has been abandoned for centuries now but it has always struck the imagination of visitors for its air of abandonment, its incredible position on the brink of the precipice and its unforgettable, romantic aura. At the far right of the bridge we start down a faint, boulder-strewn trail and carefully hike down to the rocky bed of a stream that is now dry. For about half an hour we walk between the high, reddish walls of the gorge, that is dotted with the dark caverns that were once the hermitages of anchorites. We are careful not to tarry too long below the friable rocks. We would like to stress that

excursions into gorges call for a certain amount of prudence and, above all, a careful evaluation of the weather conditions before beginning, since rain and bad weather can create dangerous situations. The vegetation of the gorge of "the Saint" is full of wild olive and carob trees. The cracks in the rocky pinnacles are home to delicate cliff-growing plants that have adapted themselves to living among the rocks. Their roots need no earth and they have tiny, delicate and colorful flowers. We gradually leave the steep cliffs of the canyon behind as the stream flows on to the sea, channeled between two narrow banks that for a hundred meters create a bizarre fjord. Our hike ends spectacularly near a natural landing made of large, red-streaked marble slabs leading down to the light blue water of the sea. Along the left-hand bank, where the earth is pleated by bands of blackish-gray rock, we discover a small natural wet dock dug into

the limestone and surmounted by an overhanging, manmade rock roof. The monks created this anchorage to ensure a haven for small boats; they would pull their boats out of the water and then climb onto dry land by means of a small ladder. Without a doubt this mooring was soon discovered and used by pirates as well and their frequent, predatory raids on the monastery eventually forced the monks to abandon it. We find this thought disturbing but are reassured by the presence of someone gathering aromatic herbs and wandering among the rocky offshoots of the gorge. The person approaches us and offers us a tender green shoot with an incomprehensible name.

Our excursion is over; we retrace our steps all the way back to the

northern span of the bridge of Katholikò, where we think we noticed
a path leading upward that is less steep. However, it proves to be just
as tricky as the original one. Before we return to Gouverneto we take
a last look at the view behind us and are reminded of the magnificent etching by a 19th century English traveler, Robert Pashley, who
was struck by the beauty of this remote site and recommended it "to
those who want to spend time far from man and in the company
of God." The feeling of profound solitude is interrupted by a happy
group of young Americans who cross our path as they head off to
repeat our experience.

Patsòs Gorge
or Saint Anthony's Gorge

 Departure point: the shrine of Agios Antonios (Patsòs)
Destination: Potami

 Hiking time: 3 hours round trip

 Level of difficulty: very challenging

 Not suitable for children

 Downhill trail

 Recommended time of the year: April to November

 Fairly well-marked trail

 Carry along a normal supply of water

Patsòs Gorge
or Saint Anthony's Gorge
The adventures of Hermes

Patsòs gorge is a perfect excursion; it can stimulate mind, hear and body. It has points of archeological interest in an extraordinar landscape and continuous challenges for excursionists who want to conquer the ravine.

From Rethimno we drive along the road to Spili that unites the two parts of the island from north to south. After 26 kilometers at Mixorouma, we follow signs for Karines and pass Labini, which has a stupendous Byzantine church dedicated to the Virgin Mar on a plateau at its outskirts. Just after Labini a road sign indicate Saint Anthony Gorge (Agios Antonios farangi), twelve kilometer away along an uphill road that offers a magnificent panorama to the south over the region of San Baseio.

When we reach the saddleback we cross into the district of Amar the first town we come upon is Karines, which is protected by Moun Kedros. Seven kilometers away is Patsòs, a village of small whit houses whose courtyards are all well-stocked with big woodpile The fountain below the roadside still serves as a washing trough as witnessed by two old women dressed in black intently scrubbin their laundry.

As we enter Patsòs, a road sign to the left indicates "Farangi Agio Antonios " and "Ravine Saint Anthony," one kilometer away. We par our car in an area shaded by an oak tree. A large wooden structur marks the entrance to the gorge and a rusti gate sets us on ou way along a gentl uphill trail protecte by a wooden railing.

We are not alone the presence of othe hikers misleads u into thinking that thi will finally be an eas gorge to explore. Bu most likely the rea reason there are s many others around i the fact that the are

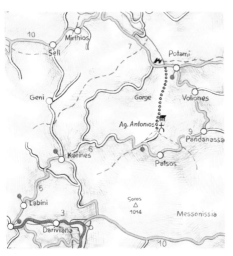

so closely resembles the romantic prints made by German artists during the 19th century: a vast, open sloping expanse with leafy, solemn plane trees leading to a gurgling stream. In recent years, in order to make the area even more enjoyable, terraces with benches have been created for enjoying the panorama and a picnic area with rustic wooden tables and a rudimental barbecue is located near an ancient fountain just a few meters from the stream. Above, in an immense grotto dug into the cliff, there is a shrine dedicated to Saint Anthony and nearby, a rocky outcropping that was once the altar of the pagan sanctuary.

Over four thousand years ago, ceremonies of the Minoan cult of nature were held here. This cult was centered on the mystery of the cycles of foliage as the seasons progressed. Divinities that are unknown to us today were propitiated with animal sacrifices and

modest offerings like oil, wine and fruit. The sanctity of the area remained intact from the Minoan era to the first centuries of the Roman conquest of the island. Special votive objects like small spear tips, sacred horns made of clay and an inscription dating back to the first century B.C. referring to the cult of Hermes Kranaeus (krane, source) were found near the altar. Hermes was venerated throughout the island as the protector of shepherds and forests and a bronze figurine was found that dates between the 1st and 3rd centuries A.D. and represents the divinity with winged sandals, pointed headgear, a quiver and a hunting trophy in his right hand. During Roman times, the adoration of Hermes was replaced by the veneration of Pan, the god of the forest, and a marble statue of this deity was also found in the vicinity.

Later, as Christianity established itself, paganism was reincarnated in the venerated figure of Saint Anthony the Hermit through a process of osmosis that was widespread throughout Crete.

We visit the small church nestled below the rock. In a corner in front of the entrance there is a collection of crutches and other votive offerings, thin pieces of metal cut in the shape of parts of the body, an arm, a leg, a head. Inside the chapel, in a room blackened by candle smoke, simple pieces of paper are lying near icons of the saint. These pieces of paper, which are also in other languages besides Greek, are personal prayers seeking a favor or giving thanks for

having been granted one.

We resume our hike at the northern edge of the forest and have to make a decision. Two wooden arrows, pointing right and left, say the same thing in Greek, "Vorio Exodo" (northern exit), and invite us to descend into the gorge. We decide to follow the eastern side of the gorge because our attention has been attracted by another sign, "Spileo Furnaro" (Furnaro grotto), a high cave dug into the rocky wall, marked with tan and pink vertical streaks that at a certain point flatten out and shade into wavy, dark gray marks.

The trail leads downward and is facilitated by wide steps made of tree trunks that are blocked in place by large, curved, iron nails. Another sign saying "Spiliares" (small caverns) leads us astray; more cavities open out under the ridge and odd concretions dangle below, stalactites over one meter long with jagged ribbing. Easy walks have been created throughout the area for people who want to enjoy nature without too much exertion, while more courageous excursionists can experience the intense emotion of taking on the gorge by following the steep hairpin turns of the path that plunges down to the bottom of the canyon. Now the floor of the ravine looks like a jumble of gigantic boulders lying next to one another and sometimes even on top of or inside one another. These massive forms seem to be elbowing each other out of the way, a rocky confusion interspersed with vegetation like the ubiquitous pink oleanders or

the slender trunks of plane trees firmly rooted in the cracks of the rocks. The trail soon ends, abandoning us; we can no longer continue along the right-hand side of the gorge. We are saved by a solid bridge with wooden parapets that leads us to the left-hand side and marks the entrance into the true ravine. From this point on we become improvised Indiana Joneses, no longer as young but just as intent on using our head, hands and feet to overcome obstacles. We climb rudimental ladders made of wood or iron that are anchored to the rock face with chains, climb through openings excavated in the rocks, and conquer other groups of boulders that lead us ever further down into the gorge. Since the fall season hasn't produced much rain yet we have the unique opportunity of crossing the gorge, which would otherwise be invaded by a rushing stream. Striking proof is given by a passage excavated under a stone arch which, with the help of a short stretch with fixed ropes, takes us into the cavea of a natural amphitheatre a few meters deep. This small lake is now dry and its uneven, black edge stands out in contrast to the pure, pearly-gray calcium deposits on the bottom. The only traces of moisture are a small, pebbly pool that is colored turquoise by the refraction of the sunbeams, and the tender, bright green foliage of maidenhair ferns clinging to the lower edge of the limestone hollow. We are now walking on the gravelly bottom of the gorge, there are no longer any trail markers, only large rocks to climb over. There are very few signs of other excursionists; we are preceded by a young, athletic hiker whose fast pace soon hides him from our view, thus preventing him from becoming a point of reference for us. The precious ladders have disappeared as well, and at a certain point we must slide down a pole, the only way to overcome yet another obstacle. We are so far down in the ravine that we only catch rare glimpses of the sky. The canyon seems like an accordion as it widens and narrows, storing hot air in its narrowest points and surrounding us with it like a bubble. After hiking for over an hour, plane trees and thorny underbrush reappear, a sign that we have conquered the gorge, and in the distance we catch a glimpse of the mighty Potami dam. We rest for a moment and then start back up the way we came. Curiously enough, the difficulty we encountered on our way down now seems minimal. The path is suffused with light, the succession of ladders leading up and down now seem like fun and we are soon back at the wooden bridge. To complete the excursion we decide to go back along the western side of the gorge, which we hadn't explored on our way down. We take a short break below the welcoming branches of a plane tree before we climb up along a well-marked trail that sometimes rises gently and sometimes is so steep that we have to use our bare hands to progress along the reddish earthen trail that hugs the pink rock face streaked with green. In fifteen minutes, after ignoring the temptation to make a detour to the edge of the stream that invitingly flows below us, or to explore yet another grotto with an unpronounceable name - "Spileo Keratokefallos" – we return to the initial fork in the trail and the chapel of Saint Anthony.

At last we abandon ourselves to a well-deserved rest in the picnic area, satisfied that we have successfully completed our small undertaking.

Roùvas Gorge

 Departure point: Lake Votomos
Destination: Roùvas forest, the church of Saint John

 Hiking time: 3 hours one way

 Level of difficulty: fairly challenging

 Not suitable for children

 Uphill trail with 540 meters vertical drop

 Recommended time of the year: April to November

 Well-marked trail with red trail markers and signs

 Carry along a sufficient supply of water

Roùvas Gorge
The perfect circle

The " farangi Roùvas " or Saint Nicholas gorge is a unique hike
that in three hours offers excursionists the pleasure of experiencing moments which many gorges have in common, a light-hearted
ascent, the challenge of complicated passages, the pure enjoyment
of pristine nature, the welcome arrival, the perfect circle of the
completed hike. The excursion starts out at a small and delightful
mountain lake, Votomos, a few kilometers from the village of Zaros.
The destination is the charming forest of Roùvas, with its rushing
streams and birdsong, high pastures, a small church made of white stones and the crown of severe mountain peaks of the Psiloriti
Mountains in the background.

On the northern side of the sweetwater lake, we carefully study the map indicating the specifics of the trail, which after a brief
ascent leads us to a wire fence delimitating the lake area. We take a
rocky path to the left that follows the western ridge of the mountain
for a quarter of an hour. After crossing a dry riverbed we reach our
first objective, the monastery of Agios Nikolaos, which is hidden by
a large, recently-built church. The monastery is modest in size and
inhabited by elderly nuns who are busily decorating the ancient,
frescoed church for the Easter ceremonies of the upcoming Holy
Week.

We resume our hike, which leads us between the slopes of two

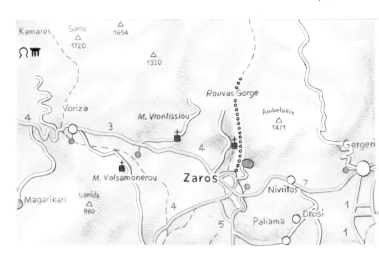

mountains, Abelakia to our right and to our left, Samari. Both mountainsides bear the scars of a forest fire that denuded the landscape of its natural foliage, leaving only thorny bushes and rock roses with their characteristic "rosebuds." We pass through a small gate and enter the true gorge; the trail's broad, easy steps are reassuring and we see the first pine tree, a sign that nature hasn't given up. The foot of the pine tree is home to sweet white cyclamens belonging to a species endemic to the island, the cyclamen creticum, which flowers in springtime. The mountain countryside seems anxious to free itself of the dead trees by pushing the carcasses down toward the valley, while higher up, pine trees and kermes oak trees with their tiny lea-

ves multiply on the slopes. The trail leads from rock to rock, grazing the ravine's walls that sometimes are of smooth, gray limestone and sometimes are ochre and black through metamorphism. We come to a path dug into the mountain that is protected by guardrails and marked with red trail markers. After an hour, our progress among the canyon's crags is halted by an immense concave cavity, a grotto whose welcoming recesses seem to invite us in to explore them. Without hesitation, we follow the flight of a bird and enter the grotto to make a brief reconnaissance. We climb over the junction of two cumbersome boulders but are forced to give up and retrace our steps when we are confronted with a second obstacle, an insurmountable wall over three meters tall rising up before us. Distracted by the imposing cave, an integral part of the gorge, we hadn't noticed that the trail makes a U-turn and protectively heads upward along the mountain ridge. Our final destination is clearly indicated on a carved wooden sign: the church of AH IANNIS- Agios Ioannis. Another sign offers us a last chance to return to our star-

ting point, passing by way of the monastery of Agios Nikolaos. Certain that the most thrilling part of the hike is still to come, we continue on along a steep path that dominates the valley, protected by a wooden railing that hugs the curving slopes, and widens out to a belvedere with a circular bench near a stream. Another hour has passed and, tempted by signs promising water and a picnic area 300 meters ahead, we only cast a quick glance at the panorama below us. We enter the ravine once again and finally find some respite from the strong sun. We cross a challenging portion of the trail among the craggy rocks and a bridge made of wide horizontal tree trunks reinfor-

ced by vertical trunks ferries us over an impassible boulder.

We are reassured to note that wise and expert people have protected and equipped the continuous crossing over from one rocky cliff side to the other with frequent and solid bridges. We soon reach a second picnic area, a circular crown of rocks that serves as a shady seat underneath a large oak tree. Roùvas gorge is full of presences and sounds, a continuous trilling of birds flying from one peak to the next, the jingling of bells around the necks of a large herd of contented, impetuous goats, an excursionist heading back down toward Votomos who can't help but tell us enthusiastically about the beautiful panoramas awaiting us. Slowly but surely we discover that the idyll is for real, Roùvas forest is pristine and dense. Its generous

and abundant streams soak the earth as they make their way among the stony ledges, creating small waterfalls and tiny mountain lakes that feed the Kermes oaks and their tiny acorns, the Holm oaks, the large leaves of the arum creticum, with their yellow spathes and dark spadixes, the frequent outcroppings of white cyclamens. We wish this portion of our hike could last forever, we stride along easily as the ravine levels out and makes room for the mountain forest. Now the trail's illustrated maps show us the fauna populating the gorge, wild cats (felix silvestris agrius), partridges, hares and barn owls. We hope to see at least one of these creatures. One more kilometer to the church; the double Minoan horns of the gray Psiloriti Mountains rise up behind the tops of the trees. The last part of the trail first leads alongside a rushing stream, then descends among the conifers and oaks. A wild pear tree curves its white flowers over the water; like magic we emerge onto a vast, grassy slope, a mountain pasture guarded by the white chapel of Agios Ioannis and a rectan-

gular building with yellow walls that serves as a shelter. In the pasture, a group of excursionists who were ahead of us have stretched out on the grass in total relaxation, even though the benches and rustic wooden tables dotting the area invite hikers to set up a well-deserved picnic.

The trail continues on over a dirt road, that is practicable with four-wheel drive vehicles, to the village of Gergeri. But we prefer to go back the way we came.

Agiofàrango Gorge

 Departure point: Odigitria Monastery
Destination: the beach at the end of the gorge

 Hiking time: an hour and a half round trip

 Level of difficulty: easy

 Suitable for children

 Downhill trail with approx. 100 meters vertical drop

 Recommended time of the year: April to November

 Well-marked trail

 Carry along a normal supply of water

Agiofàrango Gorge
The gorge of the hermit saints

It is Palm Sunday and we reach the monastery of Odigitria – de
dicated to the Virgin "who shows the way" – after leaving the villag
of Siva, where we had spent the night. The parking area in front o
the convent-fortress is full of cars; we decide to visit the monaster
later when there will be fewer people and drive down a white roac
in the direction of Kali Limenes and the coast of the Libyan sea. Afte
two and a half kilometers, on the right a sign indicates "Agiofàrango
– the gorge of the saints. This unpaved road leads down to a hollow
with drab constructions made of cement and tin sheeting that ar
used as sheep pens. We drive on for another kilometer, passing b
chained dogs with imploring gazes, until we reach the spur of th
gorge, where we leave our car in a parking lot.

As we read the information on a signboard, we discover that no
only is Agiofàrango an excursion through rocky crags that leads tc
the sea, the gorge also has mystical powers because over the centuries it has been chosen by hermits as their spiritual headquarters.

It is the middle of April, the sun is veiled and the wind is hot. A
half-hour hike takes us to our departure point, which is marked by
an iron gate that is meant to keep intrusive sheep and goats out
We open the gate and reverently enter the small ravine, anxious tc

xperience the mystical aura. Throughout the forty-five minutes of
he hike, a trickle of water continues to cross the trail and mingle
vith the stream. Lush, pink oleanders patrol the riverbanks and only
bandon us as we near the beach.

The first part of the trail leads between the narrow, wavy walls of
ed, stratified rock, which slowly widen out and reveal an abundance
f deep caves on both sides of the ravine. Hermits used to retire to
hese grottos to pray and meditate in solitude, a mute, uninterrup-
ed presence from the dawn of the second millennium to the twen-
ieth century – a practice encouraged by the climate of this canyon,
year-round haven for birds. Even today, Agiofàrango is filled with
irdsong as birds incessantly glide from one perch to another. Legend
as it that these birds are the incarnation of the souls of hermits

wandering through the gorge. The ravine is decorated with bouquets of flowers blooming in the cracks in the rocks. Cretan Ebony - ebenus cretica, endemic to the island, with its pink inflorescence and silver plumes; the violet stars of petromarula pinnata, the yellow flower of linum arboretum. Between the banks of the stream, precious silt nourishes the longevity of enormous olive and carob trees with their tangles of roots. Arum creticum white arums with elegant, cone-shaped corollas – poke out from the vegetation. We walk along the riverbed, a wide, arid path strewn with large rocks. Every now and then we make a detour to follow a faint track that wanders among the bushes on the eastern bank. To our left, the craggy rocks reveal broad slabs of gray limestone, which some young people are using for rock-climbing practice. We pause to watch one of them, the prudent placement of the rock climbing bolts, the practiced gesture of passing the double rope through the carabiners and the uneven ascent as the climber's companions on the ground carefully look on and give advice. We pass a clearing full of oleanders and reach the sacred fulcrum of the gorge, a broad open space with the beautiful church of St. Anthony, the patron saint of hermits. This is no votive chapel hidden among the grottos, this is a majestic construction surmounted by a cupola dating back to the 14th-15th century. Its longitudinal nave is nestled between two transversal naves and the intersections contain two small cupolas that are bright red, like the central dome. We enter the church through the portal, which is surmounted by an ogive arch; inside, an altar has

been dug into the rock, the original nucleus of the ancient construction. Outside, a short distance from the southern wall, several colorful tents are lined up and a few scouts are getting water from a well with a bucket tied to a long cord, while their lunch is being set up a bit further back. To the north, another rock climber is at work among the high, furrowed peaks that cast their shadows on the church. His hands are white with the climbing chalk he is using to ensure a better grip and, more daring than the previous climbers, he is about to undertake a solitary climb. He ascends for a dozen meters, swings around a stalactite hanging down from the cliff, and then continues climbing until he reaches the upper edge of the rock face, roughly sixty meters higher up. We are enchanted by the ability of this bearded climber and apprehensively watch him because he strikes us as being just a tad reckless. But who knows, maybe he is under the protection of the local saint.

The gorge has come to an end; its cliff sides are just half as tall now, leaving only rocky outcroppings. The streambed has widened out enormously; it has reached the sea and turned into a beach. Near the sandy shore, the landscape is dotted with other grottos that are ample and accessible enough to shelter human beings. A few grottos are marked with large black crosses, one even features a hieratic image drawn in charcoal. The wide pebbly beach is protected by two high barriers along the coastline. On the western side, a pinnacle rises to the sky and the daring overhang of another pinnacle leans out over the sea, forming an unusual arch. The emerald water tempts us into an early, salty baptism of the season. First we dip one foot in, then the other, but the piercingly cold water quickly sends us back to shore. We remain a bit longer on the beach; the return trip will be short, another forty-five minutes hiking under the implacable midday sun. The walls of the canyon are still festooned with rope

nd echo with the voices of the rock climbers. The priestly solitude
ve had thought we would find has been vivaciously swept away by
he vital energy of the young people. We drive back to the fortified
onvent of Odigitria and enter the deserted, silent courtyard. The
hurch's portal is framed by two palm branches, the solid, ancient
ower made of dark stone has a large embrasure through which the
nonks, in a last, desperate, defensive maneuver, threw boiling oil
own onto the heads of the Turkish invaders who had arrived by
ea.

Ròzas Gorge

 Departure point: the village of Gonies
Destination: the village of Kera

 Hiking time: 90 minutes one way

 Level of difficulty: easy with a few challenging points

 Not suitable for children

 Uphill trail with approx. 300 meters vertical drop

 Recommended time of the year: April to November

 Well-marked trail with signs

 Carry along a normal supply of water

Ròzas Gorge
Where vultures dare

Our exploration of Ròzas gorge came about in a casual and unex
pected way because our original plan had been to go for a hike ir
the gorge of Gonies. Leaving Malia and driving in the direction of the
Lassithi plateau, after ten kilometers we come upon a crossroads and
descend toward a plain in which excavations are busily underway fo
the construction of a large artificial reservoir. We reach Gonies and
as is our wont, we search for a local person who can give us mor
detailed information. We discover, to our great disappointment, tha
the entire canyon can be driven through by car. Our interlocutor, a
farmer with a sun-burnt face, consoles us by suggesting an alterna
tive excursion, the "farangi Ròzas" – the pink gorge. Just outside the
village we turn left at the "Ammos Ceramic Workshop" and follow
the wooden arrows for two kilometers until we reach the beginning
of this small ravine wedged into the folds of the gorge of Gonies, ir
which we have irremediably lost interest. Ròzas proclaims its impor
tance with a signboard featuring a map of the area, a few indication
regarding its practicability and level of difficulty, "fairly easy if th
excursionist is in good shape," a note on the botanical species pre
sent and the customary - and apt - request to respect the wildlife

This area is a
land of goats
there are pen
everywhere
we open th
wide-mesl
fencing tha
bars the en
trance to th
trail and clos
it again be
hind us. W
hike throug
a stand of oa
trees, the
the trail lead
us for abou
ten minute
along the dr

...ed of a winter stream, among oleanders and the yellow and green umbrella-like inflorescence of succulent leaves of seafennel - chritnum maritimum. We are roughly 300 meters above se level and continue upward along the wide rocky steps, accompanied by frequent groupings of dracunculus vulgaris - dragon arum. These flowers are flaunting their summer plumage; their dramatic violet bracts have been transformed into flashy cobs striped with green, yellow and red. A high wall of wavy, metamorphic rock looms above us to our right; the sunlight brings out the fuchsia tones of the rock, revealing the origin of the gorge's name. There is a solitary, inaccessible grotto halfway up the rock face; inside we can see two formations of stagmites and a rope mysteriously hanging from the roof of the cave. After half an hour the gorge narrows and the trail continues along a hollow in the rock. We are protected by a wooden railing; below us, a chasm. We come upon another clearing with oak trees and listen

to the crackling sound of acorns beneath our feet and the rustling of wings as a large bird is frightened by our passage and takes flight. Above us, among the rocky peaks, large birds of prey that nest in this area are on patrol, gyps fulvus – griffon vultures. The birds quickly plunge toward the valley bottom in search of quarry; then they rapidly ascend once again, drawing large circles in the air. The clear sky is crowded with other, less aggressive birds: young Eleonora's falcons - falco eleonorae making their first attempts at flight and timidly trying one or two circles in the air as,

suspended and immobile, they let themselves by transported by the wind before they quickly return to their haven among the rocky spires. After half an hour, we go through another rudimental iron gate and come upon our first obstacle, a miniature, circular amphitheater made of smooth rock, whose stairs we climb. Without a doubt, the rainy season transforms this drop, which is a few meters high, into a spectacular waterfall. Once we reach the stony platform above, a sign written on the wall informs us that our destination is only a kilometer away. Another modest climb and we enter an area of damp

underbrush that is full of vine-infested shrubs. A rudimental picnic area has been created here with two long, rectangular boulders placed at right angles to each other. We seem to be at the end of our excursion because our passage is now blocked by a gully, but then we see our final destination, a wooden belvedere at the top of the rocky mountain. We are rather perplexed since the vertical drop seems fairly imposing, but wooden parapets - that are actually in fairly bad shape - and a hint of

a path climbing the mountain in hairpin curves convince us to continue on. Above us, we can already see the clear outlines of the massive, ancient windmills of the "Seli Ambelou" pass, one of the historical entrances to the Lassithi plateau. We recommend that excursionists be very careful when attempting this final, very steep portion of the trail. But once they reach the belvedere their efforts will be rewarded by the sweeping vista of the valley floor. We allow ourselves time for a quick snack. We are now at 600 meters above sea level and it has taken us an hour and a half to get here. Remembering the difficul-

ty we encountered during the final part of the hike, we decide not to go back down into the gorge. We walk through a woody area for a few hundred meters and then, on our left, we glimpse the first houses of the village of Kera. In a welcoming tavern we ask how we can return to the beginning of

Ròzas gorge. A group of elderly people, who are sitting and enjoying their first raki of the day, after a brief confabulation with the owner of the tavern advise us to go to the nearby monastery of Kera Kardiotissa and from there take the white road leading to Gonies passing by way of "Apotyposis." It is already one o'clock, the sun is beating mercilessly down on the stones of the convent, insinuating its way among the whitewashed cells, invading the flowering hedges and the small courtyard in front of the main church, and tempting us to take a break in this ancient monastery-fortress and venerate the miraculous icon of the Virgin Kardiotissa. This holy image has a turbulent history. It was stolen for the first time in 1498 by a Cretan wine merchant and, after various adventures at sea, was taken to Rome and conserved in the church of Sant'Alfonso in the Esquiline district of the city. But the people of Crete, many of whom come here every year to venerate the icon on September 8th, prefer to believe the local legend. According to this legend, the icon was stolen by the Turks and reappeared at the monastery after having miraculously "fled" from Constantinople, together with the column and the chain that had shackled it in place. Today, the column is located in the courtyard in front of the church, protected by an iron fence, and

the chain is safeguarded inside the church, next to the icon.

After this interlude, we resume our hike, this time following a double sign that indicates Gonies and "Apotyposis" along a wide, easy, unpaved road that borders a fertile, verdant valley alternating low, rounded hills with rocky peaks. After a quarter of an hour, we come upon a rocky outcropping that protects the chapel dedicated to "Panagia Theotokou." This is where the Virgin, as she was fleeing Constantinople, is supposed to have rested, leaving her imprint - "apotyposis" - in the rock. From this point on the road descends rather monotonously to the valley of Gonies and after a good hour and a half, we return to our starting point at the beginning of the pink gorge.

Kritsà Gorge

 Departure point: Kritsà
Destination: the end of the gorge

 Hiking time: 1 ½ hours round trip

 Level of difficulty: easy

 Suitable for children

 Uphill trail with approx. 200 meters vertical drop

 Recommended time of the year: April to November

 Well-marked trail

 Carry along a normal supply of water

Kritsà Gorge
The archetype of gorges

We live in the region of Lassithi and one of our first excursions was to the enchanting gorge of Kritsà.

From Aghios Nikolaos, the road leads into the hills, bordering a green sea of olive trees all the way to the first houses of Kritsà, which rests gently on a hillside in a favorable position that offers a glimpse of the gulf of Mirabello. Kritsà is an ancient town; under Venetian domination it had five thousand inhabitants, an important mansion-fortress or archontika, and numerous churches. One church in particular, Panagia Kera, has precious frescos that are considered some of the most beautiful in all of Crete. Today, in the small square which is the heart of the town, there are kafenion under the plane trees which provide shade and respite from Crete's hot summer. There are also pleasant shops selling local products like thyme honey, mountain herbs, artwork carved out of olive wood, mats woven in red, yellow, green and black, and leather goods like the typical, "minimalist" summer sandals and the traditional black boots which are still worn by local farmers during the winter months.

Just before the village, to the north a large rift in the mountain marks the "farangi Kritsàs." The road curves to the right in the direction of the Lato archeological site, which a road sign indicates in very large lettering, while smaller lettering on another sign points toward the gorge. Half a kilometer further on, another sign puts us on a sheep track that leads to our departure point. No sign indicates the trail into the gorge but intuition leads us in the right direction, as we

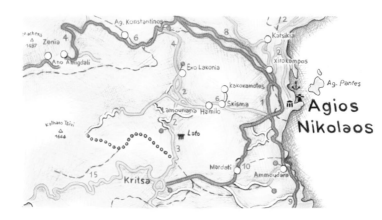

descend among vegetable gardens and vineyards to a dry riverbed. A few rough meters clambering among the rocks and then, almost as though to dissuade us from continuing on, we come upon the excursion's one obstacle, a massive boulder. But it is easily overcome after a brief and simple climb. We step over a downtrodden wire fence and disappear into the scrub that conceals the entrance of the actual ravine. Once again, we have the sensation of magical anticipation that overcomes us every time we start on a new hike, a powerful alchemy that feeds our desire to learn and discover. The first rains of November seem to have revitalized the green leaves of the oleanders and chastetree shrubs that invade the stony trail; the first white crocuses - crocus boryi peek out from the cracks in the rocks.

The trail climbs gently between low plane trees and carob trees, then leads into thick underbrush that is alive with the twittering and rusting of birds. But step by step, as we progress nature falls silent. The gorge makes its appearance as its rocky walls rise up and narrow, forcefully emphasizing their primordial material, compact, smooth rock faces that fold over on themselves in sinuous forms. We spend an intense half hour of absolute enchantment as we advance through this archetype of all gorges in miniature, as it cradles us in a pearly, limestone embrace. For roughly fifteen meters our hands are busy and our legs are tense as we cross a slippery rock face, but the incline isn't steep and the risks

are minimal. Further on, the canyon's smooth walls of white limestone almost touch, welcoming ramparts similar to opaque marble molded by a myriad of tiny rivulets that fall from above, insistently dripping and forming pools of water. The absolute solitude amplifies the magic of the surroundings and we feel like the sole privileged witnesses of such beauty. After ten minutes, the gorge widens out just as quickly as it had narrowed. The path returns, gradually leading upward along the gravel. We are surmounted by high rocky pinnacles and we make a game of trying to interpret their strange

shapes. Soon the ravine becomes less deep; it flattens out and its ridges become rounder, transforming themselves into high embankments crowned with thick stands of oak trees with narrow leaves, while below, the first autumn mushrooms hide among the tangled brambles. A good hour has passed since we began our hike. A tall pine tree blocks our way and then, further ahead, another, even taller pine tree leads us into a vast olive orchard. From here on Kritsà gorge has no further significant elements, but we continue along the riverbed until we reach the offshoots of Mount Katarò Tsivi. We make our way among olive trees along an easy incline, keeping to

the right, until we come to an unpaved cart road. After about twenty minutes the track intersects the paved road that leads upward in the direction of Tapies, and downward takes us back to where we left our car. Even though the hike was full of emotions, it was an easy and unchallenging excursion. Thus, it seems proper that we complete it with a visit to Lato, an ancient Dorian town located in the saddleback of the high hillside in front of us. We had explored the site during our first years in Crete. Back then it could still be visited all year long since there were no barriers or entrance tickets to be bought, and all one had to do was open a rudimental gate and walk upward along its cyclopean walls to the agora. This small square, whose northern side is embellished with a series of amphitheater-like steps, was the heart of the city, which dominated the entire surrounding valley, all the way to Aghios Nikolaos - Lato Pros Kamara, and beyond the sea toward the Dikti mountain range. To the south, a small temple dedicated to Apollo is located on a terrace supported by a wall. One spring, as we were sitting near the altar under the almond trees, we met a middle-aged woman who looked like farmer. She was accompanied by two foreign workers whose job it was to gather the fruit from the trees. With a confident manner, our interlocutor made a sweeping gesture with her hand, indicating the entire archeological area and the surrounding land. Noting with satisfaction our admiration for the loveliness of the area, she laid claim to the archeological site!

Saràkino Gorge

 Departure point: the village of Mithi
Destination: the end of the gorge

 Hiking time: 2 hours round trip

 Level of difficulty: fairly challenging

 Not suitable for young children

 Uphill trail with approx. 300 meters vertical drop

 Recommended time of the year: summer – July, August, September

 Well-marked trail

 Carry along a normal supply of water

Saràkino Gorge
The fun of adventure

"Saràkinos" was a term the Byzantines used to describe the Arab in reference to their brown skin. The name of this gorge, "Saràkino Saracen," takes us back in time to the end of the first millennium from 824 to 921, when Andalusian Arabs from the city of Cordova settled in Crete and made it a base for their pirate raids on the neighboring islands. Since this ravine is so close to the southern coast line we like to imagine that it was used as a secret hiding place for their booty. This motivation, a search for hidden treasure, adds three young excursionists – eight, ten and eleven years old - to our group of hikers.

Because of the great quantity of water that rushes through the gorge, Saràkino can only be explored in the summertime, when the stream calms down, insinuates itself silently into the subsoil and manifests its vitality only through the spontaneous vegetation along its riverbed: thick, aromatic leaves of myrtle, flowering oleander, small oases of cane thickets, plane trees, fig trees, chastetree shrubs. Our best moment for discovering the gorge is a day in mid-July. We drive toward the southeastern part of the island, past Ierapetra, in the direction of Mirtos, a pleasant seaside town which strives to make visitors forget the overbuilt outskirts of Ierapetra and the unremitting disfigurement of the surrounding countryside by the om-

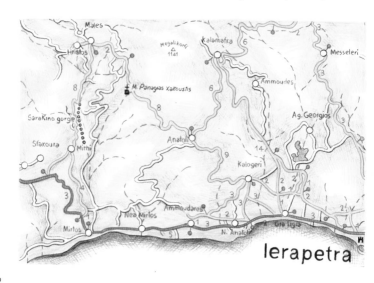

ivorous presence of hothouses. From Mirtos, we continue toward
he southern outcroppings of the Dikti mountain range, passing by
rid sandstone coves. After a few kilometers we reach Mithi and
ery evident arrows indicate a road which takes us to our departure
oint. In the parking area there are various cement structures of the
ocal waterworks and a tavern, "Saràkino," which is now shuttered
nd abandoned.

In the beginning, we teeter along the low walls of the water
nains, cross a rudimental, shaky bridge, and continue along a path
hat edges a rift between two gigantic walls of gray limestone. This
pectacular, concave foyer gives excursionists the feeling of being
nside the rocky home of Titans, where an incredible variety of bi-
arre landscapes have been created by unfettered Nature. Gigantic
oulders balancing one on top of another, grottos excavated into
ndulated rock by wild metamorphism, secret passages created insi-
e the rocks, a growing number of marvels, leading up to the gorge's
riumphant entrance with its immense, rocky arch.

We are a lively group of hikers and we worry whether we will be
ble to ensure the safety of the children in our group, if we can rein
n their enthusiasm in the most difficult sections without dimini-
hing their spirit of adventure. Even though the scarcity of water in
he summer has eliminated the problem of having to wade across
ifficult parts of the stream, strong arms and light feet will be nee-
ed in order to cross some of the boulders.

We proceed cautiously, taking care to stay near the rock walls

to avoid any stones that might be knocked loose by a group of goats that have found their way into the gorge above us in search of grass. Our point of reference is the streambed, whose irregular flow sometimes widens, sometimes narrows. There are no trail markings and we are basically wandering among the huge, scattered boulders, cumbersome presences that will frequently halt our progress as we search for the best solutions for continuing on. We cross our first obstacle with the help of a rickety wooden ladder which is missing

its top rungs. The situation is becoming increasingly worrisome; it is as though angry giants had tossed enormous marbles every which way. One of these huge round rocks has even gotten stuck between the walls of the gorge and balances menacingly in mid-air. We pass underneath natural stone arches, we squeeze between narrow passages where the water has polished the limestone to perfection, we pass over small rocky hillocks with the

help of our hands, a careful positioning of our feet in the cracks, and the precious assistance of the strongest member of our group. As agile as cats, the youngest excursionists scramble their way lightly up over the obstacles with the derring-do of those who don't know the meaning of danger. For them, the highpoint of the hike is an adventurous passage inside a large cave with a short, narrow tunnel that requires a few contortions before emerging into a small clearing. Since the children are the first to go through the tunnel, they help the "grownups" through, with amused comments about the heft of each one of us and the awkwardness with which we pass this test.

After hiking for almost an hour, the gorge becomes friendlier and we pick up the trail once again. The path becomes increasingly more damp until we come upon trickles of water. Among the ferns and moss we have a surprising encounter with a large sweetwater crab

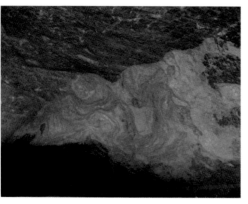

that is half hidden beneath the flat stratum of a rocky recess. It is a Potamon Fluviatile, a crustacean that belongs to an ancient family of crabs. These creatures live in sweet and brackish water inside burrows they dig that can be up to one meter deep they eat worms, seeds and acorns. Our crab's wide-spaced, round, bluish eyes poke up from its square shell that is a lovely shade of yellow with violet and dark crimson highlights. It stares at us diffidently. One of us, courageous and expert firmly picks it up, holding its formidable claws shut. The children are amazed and excited by this discovery, the crab is motionless; it seems dazed so we splash a bit of water on it. Once we have released it, it waves its long, hooked claws and slowly backs its way into its hiding place. One hundred meters higher up, a pool of water, the first we

have come upon, reassures us as to the crab's survival. We are at the end of the gorge, the vast opening of the exit is just as imposing and solemn as the entrance and leads us into thick underbrush traversed by a rivulet that is still weak and irregular. We have been hiking for over an hour; in front of us fields, olive orchards and vineyards re-appear. A brief picnic and we decide to return the way we came. The trail leads downhill now and we imitate our young hiking compa-nions and let ourselves slide down the long, stony ledges that are as smooth as marble. A few meters from the end of our hike we come upon a couple of Germans wearing protective helmets, climbing ro-pes draped around their necks. They ask us about the accessibility of the trail and tell us that three years earlier they had been forced to swim across certain portions of the gorge because the water was neck-high! We later learn from local excursionists that the gorge always has a few points that must be swum across and that this year it was dry only because the water had been deviated higher up. We don't know if this is only temporarily or permanently.

Orinò Gorge

Departure point: Koutsouras Park
Destination: four kilometers from the village of Orinò

Hiking time: 3 hours one way

Level of difficulty: easy

Suitable for children (only the first part of the excursion)

Uphill trail with 250 meters vertical drop

Recommended time of the year: April to November

Trail with yellow and red trail markers

Carry along a normal supply of water

Orinò Gorge
The butterfly gorge

The Orinò massif is pierced by a vertical gash, the result of thou
sands of years of erosion. Until a few years ago it had been covere
by a luxuriant forest of pine trees which well suited the name "daso
gorge," the forest gorge. Today, the forest has been swept away by
terrible forest fire and it has returned to its geological denomination
"Orinò gorge" or, more romantically, the "butterfly gorge." We wi
come upon many of these lepidopterans in the wet oases and th
underbrush as we hike along the stream that traverses the gorge.

Excursions in this polyhedral canyon can be adapted to the streng
th and intentions of the hiker. An hour of pleasant walking lead
to the first check-point, the small church of Saint Demetrios, afte
which the tenacity of the excursionist is put to the test by an uphi
hike lasting another two hours. But perseverance is rewarded by stu
pendous vistas and the constant presence of abundant waterfall
We start our hike at the Koutsoura nature reserve, which is locate
along the road from Ierapetra to Makrighialos. A kilometer befor
Makrighialos, Koutsoura Park is clearly marked on the left. The par
has hectares of reforested land, a vast clearing that serves as a par
king lot and a refreshment area with a lovely wooden chalet wit
benches and tables under the pine trees. An oleander-lined road take
us toward the folds of the mountain; after walking for ten minute
near a large, blue tube marked IGME, a waterworks breather pipe, th
trail becomes narrower and wends its way among the first boulder
As we hike uphill, the view is ruined by the sad spectacle of the clif
sides that were devastated by a forest fire in 1993, sad and oppressiv

vidence of human error. But, amazingly, this desolate landscape car-
es within itself the seeds of its future catharsis: near the shattered
rees, others are miraculously rising up intact with thick foliage. New,
mid shoots of life peep out from the ground, miniature pine trees,
lready straight and proud, and shiny green saplings of small kermes
ak trees - quercus coccifera.

The trail is often blocked by enormous tree trunks but in the con-
nuous ups and downs of the trail there is vitality and lush greenery
long the streambed. Aromatic bushes of oregano, sage and thyme,
hrubs of rock roses and mastic trees, a profusion of white and fu-
hsia oleanders, all reveal the powerful will of nature to carry on. The
avine is never monotonous, it rises among the recesses of the rocky
valls; it leads back downward into small oases of vegetation - the

first chastetrees with their violet spicae, pungent tufts of wild asparagus, broad aromatic fig leaves – and is fed by modest trickles of water that slip along the limestone and aren't yet able to transform themselves into a proper waterfall. Only in one point is our passage blocked by a boulder, an impediment which is easily surmounted with the help of a wooden ladder that leads solidly and safely up for a few meters. A young couple with two children ahead of us are able to overcome the obstacle without difficulty.

After hiking for half an hour we come upon a hollow that is completely overgrown by a cane thicket. A light wind shakes the cane causing a subdued jangling noise; the only real sound is the characteristic call of the partridges which are disturbed by our presence and rise heavily into the air from the underbrush to find refuge in the inaccessible crags. A brief climb and we find ourselves underneath an enormous, ancient pine tree, whose twisted branches create a natural arch and offer respite from the strong sun. The canyon wall

have narrowed, the red trail markers, which have helped us follow the right path, herd us in single file along the uncomfortable cement wall of the waterworks, leading to a rural setting of olive orchards and cultivated vegetable patches. After a good hour's hike the first part of our excursion is over; we are near the whitewashed chapel dedicated to Saint Demetrios. We rest near the belvedere in front of the church,

with its stone fountain, long table and wooden benches. The fountain promises fresh water but we are unable to make it work. From a nearby field, a farmer comes to our rescue. He is accompanied by a boy who is around six or seven years old, with whom we share some dried figs and chocolate snacks. We visit the chapel, which appears to be very old. The external lunette has a painting of Saint Demetrios in armor astride a bay horse, about to lance an infi-

el who our Cretan interlocutor promptly identifies as a "Turk." Inside the chapel there are a great many icons dedicated to the saint, whose name is often accompanied by the attribute "stereanos" – he who watches over the prosperity of fruit trees, the abundance of harvests and the multiplication of flocks. We can't help but associate the name

Demetrios - or Demetrius, Diocletian's martyr - with Demetra, the Greek goddess of fertility, who the people of Crete believe was born here, and note how the osmosis between sacred and profane is still very present in the Greek-Orthodox religion.

We resume our hike among the olive trees on a well-cultivated plateau. Below, the local farmers have planted vegetables along the banks of the rushing stream. The trail continues to lead upward and stops at a small wooden bridge that daringly rests on a high cement wall and connects the

two banks, that would otherwise remain separated. Bright yellow arrows peremptorily conduct us downhill through a small thicket of brambles to the left bank of the torrent. For a quarter of an hour we have no other choice than to wade, sometimes with our hiking boots immersed in the water, sometimes balancing on the uneven rocks in the stream as we steady ourselves by holding on to the flexible canes of the rushes. The yellow trail markers have disappeared and have been substituted by red spots that advise hikers to avoid following the increasingly impetuous water of the stream and to begin hiking

urther up on the left-hand side of the canyon. We savor the pleasure of hiking uphill and down, often ending up in picture-perfect oases with sandy bottoms, small waterfalls with smooth stones, shady plane trees, an abundance of violet campanulas, and the tall stalks of Bear's Breeches - acanthus spinosus mollis which inspired the ornamental motifs of the Corinthian capitals in ancient Greece. Finally we sight the vivid colors of the first butterflies. After an hour we reach an abandoned dam, a tall, smooth platform green with moss

that is barely veiled with water. Higher up, the peak of Mt. Askordalia is clearly outlined against the sky. In a few points the trail becomes tricky and very steep, the protective guardrails of the only forested portion, with its tall, solitary pine trees, have disappeared. For a brief stretch the ridge offers few handholds, only a couple of large stones and the crumbly earth, but it is only for a moment. Soon the canyon relaxes and our destination is at hand; just beyond the ravine to the left is the high, safe, paved road leading to the mountain village of Orinò. Undergrowth redolent of myrtle hides a vigorous waterfall from view, but guided by the sound of the water we penetrate the vegetation until we come upon a rocky hollow that slows the impetus of the water, imprisoning the waterfall for a moment in a deep pool before releasing it and funneling it through a round hole in the rock. After two hours of hiking, a barbed-wire fence explicitly marks the end of the excursion.

Pefki Gorge

 eparture point: Pefki
Destination: the end of the gorge

 Hiking time: 2 hours round trip

 Level of difficulty: a few difficult points

 Not suitable for children

 Downhill trail with approx. 200 meters vertical drop

 Recommended time of the year: April to November

 Trail with signs that aren't always very visible

 Carry along a normal supply of water

Pefki Gorge
The perfume of maritime pines

From a geological point of view, Pefki gorge is not considered one of the thirty-four "official" gorges on the island of Crete. The chasm king of this area is without a doubt the dramatic "Ha canyon" in the nearby Tripti mountain range. But we aren't mountain climbers and, thus, conquering that dangerous, perpendicular cleft is an impossible undertaking for us. It's better to make do with hiking through this natural hollow, whose special charm is offered by the constant presence of pine trees that inebriate us with their perfume and accompany us on this short hike that isn't without surprises. We are on the south-eastern coast at Makrighialos, roughly thirty kilometers from Ierapetra, and turning our backs on its beautiful beach, we head inland toward the mountain. After seven kilometers we see the village of Pefki stretching out along the slopes of a vast plateau which juts up naked and cone-shaped to the south, surmounted by the white chapel of Stavromenos - the Holy Cross. In the village we stop our car next to an elderly farmer intent on loading bundles of wood into his decrepit pickup truck and ask him how to reach the entrance to the gorge. The farmer sizes us up with an eloquent glance and observes that the gorge is for young people, ironically expressing his doubts as to our ability to survive the hike. Our pride is piqued and we insist; after being given the directions, we drive to the edge of the village, where we find a board with a detailed map of

the area and the hiking time.

Our hike starts along a wide and very clear, unpaved road that leads between vegetable patches and massive olive trees and brings us to a fork in the trail. Another sign and red trail markers direct us to the right, along a path lined with bushes of rock roses, chastetrees and myrtle until we reach four majestic, soaring pines. We continue on for another three hundred meters to the substantial ruins of ancient windmills that are suffocated by a tangle of vegetation. From this height we enjoy a magnificent view of the spurs of the ravine, whose high, smooth walls of stratified rock nestle in the valley bottom in a thick forest of pine trees. The infinite horizon of the Libyan Sea and the hazy outlines of the villages of Makrighialos and Analipsi can be seen in the distance. We keep to the western edge of hillside, facing out over the deep valley; on the hillside in front of us, to the east, there are many traces of a recent forest fire. We come upon

another fork in the trail, a dry well, a map and three wooden arrows, one of which indicates "Piso Kamino" - high road - to the left, while the other two indicate "farangi" and " gorge," respectively.

The path, which is marked by the globular stalks of sea-onions, a herald of the imminent autumn, plunges into the gorge in a steep and rapid descent, escorting us down to its nucleus, which is traversed by a small stream struggling its way among the rocks. Initially, we must squeeze between the slightly creased walls of metamorphic rock, in which the pressure of thousands of years has opened high fissures of schistose stone. We come upon light green stands of majestic pine trees, the absolute and ubiquitous protagonists of our excursion. Botanically, the Greek word "pefko" corresponds to the Latin word pinus brutia or, more commonly, maritime pine, a tree with a straight trunk, aciform leaves and curved pine cones. A generous plant, in ancient times it was consecrated to Poseidon, the god of the sea, because it furnished the best wood for building the hulls of ships. Today, its sap produces retsina, a dry white wine with

a characteristically sharp and aromatic flavor.

This forest of conifers doesn't leave much room for a wide variety of flowers, but in the springtime it isn't unusual to find surprising and multicolored orchids, ophrys lutea or episcopalis, tiny and sumptuous in the contrast of their yellow labellum speckled with brown and purple; and red orchis quadripunctata, up to thirty centimeters tall and suffused with pink inflorescence. The trail follows the sinuous outline of the ravine, descending to its floor among large rocks that group together and create small sandy oases invaded by oleanders and chastetree bushes, and then leading upward again, protected by wooden guardrails overlooking the precipice, as forests of plane trees and small oak trees make their appearance. After three quarters of an hour of hiking our physical condition is put to the test as we come upon an insidious barrier of conglomerate boulders that

challenge our ability to find the best way out; with sure hands and steady feet we search for the best hand- and footholds. After overcoming this obstacle we set off once again along the trail that leads up along the western side of the gorge, protected from the chasm below by guardrails. Suddenly the trail ends, it no longer exists, only a small ledge sticking out horizontally from the rocky wall protects us from a drop of several meters. We

must climb down an iron ladder with seventeen rungs, the last two of which are rickety and shaky. The feeling of precariousness is so strong, the chasm below is so unwelcoming, that we decide to turn our backs to it and descend the ladder facing the rocky wall. We reach the bottom safe and sound, but a few meters later we find ourselves in the same situation as before. Another series of ladders that are less hazardous and in better condition than the first one takes us to the final portion of the canyon, with blackberry bushes, ferns and maidenhair ferns in a mossy, green pond. We soon come upon a paved road that leads in the direction of Makrighialos. Since we are stubborn and not yet satisfied by the brief journey, we are tempted to follow a path on the left-hand side of the road that is marked by vegetation and that seems to be an appendix of the gor-

ge. For a quarter of an hour we try to descend, guided by the black rubber tubes of the waterworks. Soon, further ahead, we hear an agitated voice, then we see people who appear to be in difficulty and seem unable to find their way out of the tangle of trees and rocks. We prudently wait for them to reach us and discover that they are a group of Poles who have clearly taken a wrong turn. One of them has a large gash on his leg. They are distressed and almost implore us not to continue along the same trail they took. For once we are judicious and return to the gorge, retracing our steps to Pefki, which takes a good hour. In town, a fresh breeze mitigates the strong, early September sun; we are ravenous and look for a traditional tavern where we can have a bite to eat. A delightful restaurant called "pipe-ri" with a wide terrace facing the sea is a pleasant discovery. We eat under the broad, drooping branches of a tree with rounded leaves and small, bright red berries. We are intrigued by the exotic aspect of the unfamiliar tree and the friendly young owner of the restaurant informs us that it is a Schinus molle or false pepper tree. A highly aromatic essential oil that smells like pepper is extracted from the tree and is used in herbal medicine. We share this moment of rela-xation with other foreign hikers who, like us, appreciate more than just the magnificent beaches of this island and love to penetrate its rocky backbone made of mountains, valleys and rifts and hike along the European long-distance hiking trail, the E4, that traverses the island from east to west.

Zakròs Gorge

Departure point: Zakròs
Destination: Kato Zakròs

Hiking time: 2 hours one way

Level of difficulty: Easy

Suitable for children

Downhill trail with approx. 200 meters vertical drop

Recommended time of the year: April to November

Well-marked trail with red trail markers

Carry along a normal supply of water

Zakròs Gorge
The valley of the dead

It took us a while before we discovered the beauty of Farangi nekron – the valley of the dead – in part because we found its funereal name vaguely disquieting and in part because we were afraid of encountering dangerous situations we couldn't control. But all it took was a 2-hour hike in this meandering ravine to dispel our fears and to discover that the gorge is named after the various Minoan tombs that have been found in its caves. The canyon, which is traversed by the Zakròs river, is located at the eastern-most edge of the island, in the district of Sitia, a remote area full of Minoan artifacts The gorge holds many surprises and the excursion can be divided into three parts that are interconnected by the purplish path leading through the canyon. This sumptuous mineral carpet is made of cuprite which has emerged from the rocky depths and unfolds beneath our feet, accompanying us to the Minoan palace of Kato Zakròs.

The first part of the excursion is the beginning of the hike just outside the village of Zakròs, among hillsides that are completely covered with vineyards. The peaks of the gorge are barely visible; we come upon the first trail sign, the symbolic iron gate to be opened and shut, the European trail logo. After ten minutes of walking downhill

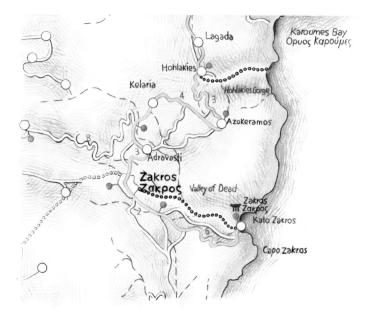

we find ourselves immersed in a wild yet pleasant landscape. We are in a clearing, deafened by the noise of a stream that rushes in, widens out into a lively pool and then continues on its way as it surges among a gallery of noble plane trees. An air of holiness wafts among these trees, with their palm-shaped leaves and bark that scales off in large patches. Ancient plane trees were venerated as a generous gift of the gods; they were the favorite trees of Jove, who lay with the nymph Europa under their foliage. In the midst of this grandiosity, we mortals find a "mauve" path leading past small rocky concretions. For about twenty minutes we repeatedly have to wade through the river and hop from one flat rock to another as we cross and re-cross

the water.

We pass by a leafy oasis full of gigantic oleanders enclosed by walls of schistose rock with deep grooves.

We climb a hillside for a meditative rest under the shade of enormous, wild olive trees. A family with two children merrily come in our direction from the lower part of the gorge; their presence is proof that there will be few challenging passages and that the constant, precise, almost imperious trail signs rule out any risk of losing our way.

The gleaming water enlivens the riverbanks with a myriad of oregano bushes; some of the clusters of capsules are still green, others have already opened, disclosing the white inflorescence with its penetrating fragrance. The further we descend, the more the water is harnessed by large, black tubes; the trail disappears and we are obliged to teeter along the narrow wall of the waterworks and squeeze past an enormous plane tree imprisoned between two blocks of stone. We stop for a drink of water at a fountain in the first picnic area. Two

wooden arrows indicate the opposite directions of the excursion, while a third, which says "Azokeramos," marks a destination along the European trail. After an hour of hiking, we enter the archeological phase of the itinerary, in which the Minoan influence is tangible. The millenary walls of Lenika, an ancient and mysterious manmade relic, can clearly be seen halfway up the archeological area, surrounded by rocky hills. The vegetation has settled at the bottom while the gorge rises up and towers above it. On the western side, above, there is an arch-shaped grotto. All of a sudden the stream hides and turns into a simple flow of water that is channeled into a cement collecting pool. We continue on in single file for a quarter of an hour, then the trail reappears along the eastern side of the ravine. When we reach the valley bottom, a sign that says Parking indicates a trail that winds up along the hillside in front of us. Another arrow pointing in the other direction simply indicates Kato Zakròs Beach. We know that the first trail leads to

another entrance of the gorge, a short road halfway between Zakròs and Kato Zakro which would have deprived us of the profound allure of the first two phases of the hike. The excursion continues along easily in an open landscape; the crags of the ravine, which are still quite high, are separated by the vast riverbed, which is obstructed with boulders and is barely fed by small streamlets. The underbrush is the realm of chastetrees, bushes of thyme and oregano, the wilted and blackish spathes of dragon arum - dracunculus vulgaris, and small populations of cuckoopint, another type of arum whose calyxes have folded over onto themselves, an indication that springtime turned into summer too quickly. Another sign informs us that the ruins of Kastelas, a Minoan sanctuary on the hilltop, await us among the rocky peaks of a 20-minute trail for experts only. We decide to forgo the hike because the trail rises up dangerously and perpendicularly along the eastern rock face. The reddish rock is very stratified and feels as though it could be riffled like the pages of a book. If only the rocks could "talk" maybe they could tell us about the people who, three or four thousand years ago, used to gather flowers for cosmetic unguents and herbs for therapeutic infusions, who kept bees, who propitiated their gods by electing the mountain peaks as sanctuaries for their rites. A plateau hides the sea from our view, but there are cavernous grottos along the ridges, in which the Eteocretans, the first inhabitants of this part of the island, buried their dead. Numerous objects have been found in the area, the most interesting of which is a magnificent cylindrical pyx with triangular decorations on its cover and a handle in the stylized shape of a crouching dog.

We are at the end of the canyon; an immense line of oleanders marks the trail, which is now level. Fine sand invades the stream; to the left, behind the hill, the cyclopean walls of the Minoan palace await us, stretched out like an amphitheater over a vast area. This immense site was untouched for thousands of years, until two Cretans who were fascinated with antiquity, a rope maker from Sitia and a fisherman/innkeeper from Kato Zakròs, guessed the location of the fourth and perhaps most complete of the island's palace-sanctuaries that have been discovered to date.

Unfortunately, it isn't possible to enter the site after three in the afternoon, so we must forgo the visit and make our way among the vegetable patches to the seashore. The bay is tranquil and we stop and enjoy the simplicity of the fare in one of the taverns lined up under the shade of the tamarisk trees.

Hohlakiés Gorge

Departure point: the village of Hohlakiés
Destination: Karoumes Bay

Hiking time: 3 hours round trip

Level of difficulty: easy

Suitable for children

Downhill trail with slight vertical drop

Recommended time of the year: April to November

Well-marked trail

Carry along a good supply of food and water

Hohlakiés Gorge
Thalassa, thalassa!

The people of Crete love to spend the first of May outdoors, and their custom is to return home from their outings with large bouquets of wildflowers that they weave into wreaths to adorn car hoods and front doors for good luck. For our celebration of the first of May we wanted to go on an easy hike that ends in glory at the seaside, where we might even go for our first swim of the season. Hohlakiés gorge seemed like the ideal excursion since it satisfies both our pleasure in studying the beauty of the geological formations in the canyons, and our yen for the sea since the gorge ends in the spectacular, rounded bay of Karoumes, at the eastern-most end of the island.

With its unpronounceable, onomatopoeic name, which might relate to the verb $\chi o \chi \lambda a \zeta \omega$ (which in Greek means to gurgle), the ravine is located near Hohlakiés, a meager agglomeration of houses seven kilometers from Paleokastro and Sitia. We cross the village without meeting a soul, but the freshly whitewashed walls and the flower pots next to the front doors indicate the presence of human beings, perhaps only a handful of elderly people stubbornly rooted to their land. This village has had its share of suffering; it was atta-

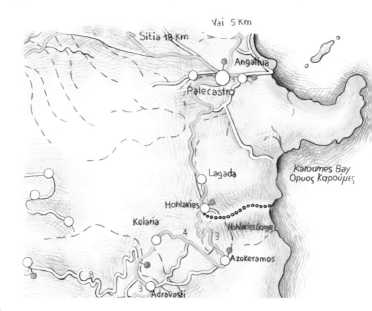

cked by the Turks and repeatedly devastated in 1821 and 1866, as witnessed by the ruins of its earliest nucleus near the low, bleak plateau of Aginaras, which faces the cleft in the mountain. An unpaved road winds its way among the olive orchards until it reaches a mandatory parking lot near a white chapel, where a sign indicates the descent into the gorge with a map of the trail and its geographical location. It takes us about twenty minutes to reach the entrance of the gorge, which is protected by a feeble fence. Despite this precaution the canyon is a land of conquest for the voracious black goats who study us from above, lined up along the rocky southern wall on the only alternative trail when the stream is in full flood and hikers cannot walk along the dry riverbed.

A still-flowering exam
ple of dragon arum - dra
cunculus vulgaris, whos
violet spathe is laced with
dark brown spots, haugh
tily marks the trail. The
we begin a gymkhana
among the loose stone
of the dry riverbed as th
omnipresent red and blu
trail markings show us th
proper direction to take
Throughout the entir
excursion we keep to th
southern side of the gor
ge, an elevated rock fac
of crystalline and mar
ly shale, whose reddis
color goes well with th
foliage of the many type
of shrubs growing in the soil. The growth of these plants has bee
influenced by the caprices of the contours of the rock face; there ar
crooked olive trees whose treetops are dangerously exposed, as we
as wild bushes that have grown haphazardly. Only the lovely campa
nula pelviformis, with their bright blue, pedunculated inflorescence
seem at ease in the rocky hollow. The first part of the hike is ofte
obstructed by boulders that are so near to each other that only th
millenary flow of the river has separated them and opened narrow

passages, shaping rudimental steps in the rocks. These imperfect but climbable stairs are a providential "deus ex machina" that in about an hour covers the entire one hundred meters of vertical drop. Hohlakiés valley proves to be an "athletic" hike because it puts the agility of hikers' ankles and the elasticity of their knees to the test. No dizzying heights, no fixed routes with swaying ropes, only muscle-testing ascents and descents. The first soft landing, in a small valley of oleanders and chastetree shrubs, gives us an excuse to stop in the shade of an old olive tree with knotty folds in its trunk. A wreath of corroded and pitted stones marks the spot where the torrential

rains gurgle forth in the wintertime, proving the etymology of the "farangi Hohlakion." In the rock face in front of us a dark cavity to the left is perforated by two gleaming eyes – just a reflection of

the sun or the silent presence of a predator? This enigma remains unsolved as we resume our hike which, once again, presents us with an obligatory passage among fairly low pinnacles and peaks. Next we cross a green jungle of oregano interspersed with insidious nettles and finally come upon chastetree bushes with their flexible and stubborn branches. Homer narrates that Ulysses tied his companions firmly underneath the belly of a ram with chastetree branches when they escaped from Polyphemus' cavern.

The crags of the ravine diminish, the jagged peaks come to an end, leaving only a few cone-shaped projections as the landscape evens out into an embroidered crest. We are certain we followed the trail markings properly but, we ask ourselves, where is the sea? An arid plateau is still hiding Karoumes Bay as our eagerness to see the marine horizon grows. Finally, the gorge veers to the left, a few more steps on the crushed stones and then a triumphant "thalassa – the sea!" echoes down the valley. A strong sirocco wind is blowing, the heat imprisoned between the rock walls lessens as we follow a path alongside the riverbank which makes its way among the thorny rotundity of Albanian spurge and shrubby kidney vetch - anthyllis hermanniae, whose golden inflorescence is filled with a light, pleasant fragrance. The blue line of the sea widens before our eyes, heralded by an arid clearing dotted with pungent tufts of Marram grass - ammophila arenaria. The circular gulf of Karoumes is swept by strong gusts of wind, there will be no swimming in that agitated water today. We are deeply disappointed that we won't be able to swim across to the flat grotto on the right-hand side of the bay. It took us an hour and a half to walk down the gorge; we decide to find shelter from the sun and wind and relax under the tamarisk tree on the opposite side, near the beautiful beach with its delicately multihued stones.

Refreshed, we don't want to waste the momentum we have acquired and thus resume our hike, preceded by a robust man equipped with spray paint and alpenstock, who is intent on touching up the trail markers with red paint. On our return trip we discover other small wonders of nature we hadn't noticed before, like a large wild olive tree twisted like a snake around a smooth, limestone outcropping; and a rock that has been carved into the shape of a gigantic seashell and creates such a lovely frame that the children accompanying us on our excursion ask to have their photograph taken inside it. Our feet fly over the successive levels as we hike back up the gorge, the exertion is minimal, we return to our departure point and open the obligatory gate.

Richtis Waterfall

 Departure point: Tigania beach (Exo Mouliana - Sitia)
Destination: Richtis waterfall

 Hiking time: 1 hour round trip

 Level of difficulty: easy

 Suitable for children

 Uphill trail with approx. 200 meters vertical drop

 Recommended time of the year: April to November

 Trail with red trail markers that aren't always visible

 Carry along a normal supply of water

Richtis Waterfall
The waterfall symphony

After tackling impervious gorges and challenging hikes, we ar
pervaded by a feeling of tranquility when we go on easy excursion
whose only goal is to admire nature without being stressed by th
final destination. To this end, an ideal short excursion is to Richti
waterfall, near Exo Mouliana, in search of a refreshing oasis to esca
pe the summer heat. Exo Mouliana is a village located in the north
eastern part of the island along the coastal road between Agic
Nikolaos and Sitia. We follow our trusty tactic of asking for infor
mation at the local café, where the men of the village are enjoyin
their Sunday in total relaxation. Some of the men are concentratin
on playing a game of tavli, while others are chatting and keepin
an eye on the weekend traffic on the national road. We interrup
their pastimes and they inform us that a small road to the left a
the outskirts of the village leads to Tigania beach, the starting poin
of the hike. Just outside the town limits we come upon leafy, culti
vated vegetable patches: large heads of endive and maruli, the sta
of many a Greek salad, are lined up next to rows of green bean:
which in turn are crowded by the broad, gray-green leaves of zuc
chinis. Chorta, a staple seasonal vegetable that must be cooked, i
relegated to the side of the vegetable patches, next to tousled tuft
of perfumed dill. This greenery disappears as we continue on an
soon the side of the road only offers exhausted, sun-faded bushes c
Jerusalem sage - Phlomis fruticosa and spiny spurge. The only plan
that seems to thrive in the heat is the caper plant, with its smal

tubborn and succulent leaves and capsule-shaped flower buds. We
ollow the hairpin turns carved into the imposing, rocky walls of the
oastline, mesmerized by the immensity of the sea that caresses the
aked spurs of the cliffs all the way to the eastern tip of the island.
Ve are fascinated by the stretch of sea glittering in the sun. At last
ve sight the objective of our excursion, a solitary, long strip of vege-
ation that starts at the sandy shore and makes its way up into the
olds of the mountain. A vast clearing shaded by tall tamarisk trees
narks the beginning of the small beach of Tigania, which seems to
ave seen better days. There are a few old army tents with camping
tensils hanging outside and a corrugated iron shed. Large stones

make entering the water complicated; the merciless sea often bring
trash to shore and among the plastic jerrycans, scorched logs, piece
of fishhooks and torn nets, we find a small glass bottle with a mes
sage inside. We can't resist and try to decipher the message, whic
is written in Greek on a piece of white paper: an indecipherable dat
and references to an ideal weight that has been reached (45 kilo
and a diet. Our unknown, aspiring Bridget Jones seems to have en
trusted an excerpt of her diary to the sea!

After leaving the beach we head inland among overgrown gra
pevines that have reached an abnormal height and triumphantly d
splay small bunches of dark grapes that look more like blackcurrant
We leave our car in the parking lot and start down a long path tha
is marked with a faded trail marker and that flanks large black pipe

The beginning of the hike isn't thrilling but an arrow encourages us to continue on, past a cement waterworks building and among the rushes of a marsh with greenish water that is swarming with insects. On the shore, hiding under a piece of hollow log on the grainy sand, we encounter a sweetwater crab - potamon fluvialis, our old friend from Sarakino gorge. We pass the ruins of a stone watermill and proceed for a good distance, surrounded by shoulder-high, thorny bushes. The ravine leads slowly upward and winds its way among low, rocky concretions to a riverbed whose banks are covered with aromatic herbs. We reach a clearing crowded with plane trees that bend over the stream and shade the water with their palmate leaves. We also see a large example of arum creticum – cuckoopint, whose heart-shaped leaves are lightly veiled in white. It feels as though we are in the middle of a small Mediterranean jungle. We are overwhelmed by this abundan-

ce of natural beauty; the polyhedral stream draws a harmonious path among the large white boulders in its bed and makes its way through the vegetation, losing itself in a myriad of streamlets until it finally seems to settle down and pause in pools of crystal clear water. Our hike continues through an underbrush of blackberry brambles, oleanders and wild olive trees, as the leaves of plane trees crackle underfoot and accompany us from one clearing to the next. There are few challenging passages, only an accumulation of large, rounded boulders requiring a brief climb. One time we have to pull ourselves up to avoid the stream, which widens out until it covers the path and become a small pool of water. This last effort takes us into an enchanted forest hiding a surprise that has yet to reveal itself but that we can already imagine. The silence has been replaced by a musical, unmistakable noise, the intense roar of Richtis waterfall. Before manifesting itself in all its glory, the waterfall requires a tribute and forces us to lower our heads to pass below the yokes and woody arches of a tangle of plane trees that are bizarrely intertwined and that lead to a vast grassy expanse.

Finally, the waterfall reveals itself; from a height of roughly thirty meters the water is filtered by brilliant moss and flows into two opposite branches. It caresses the rocky walls, it climbs over the ivy, it overwhelms the delicate maidenhair fern hidden underneath a recess, it dives down and joyously widens out. It is an unexpected spectacle for a late-August day in Crete and it inspires us to action. We are tempted to find a way to climb up and circumvent the waterfall, to understand where it comes from, to discover what is hidden beyond it. A narrow but steep track rising on the right-hand side of the ravine entices us. But we are prudent and don't want our easy

one-hour hike to turn into an enterprise, so we content ourselves
with admiring the splendor before us and then retrace our steps
back to our starting point.

Pervolàkia Gorge

 Departure point: near Kapsa monastery
Destination: the village of Pervolàkia

 Hiking time: 2 hours one way

 Level of difficulty: moderately challenging

 Not suitable for children

 Uphill trail with approx.400 meters vertical drop

 Recommended time of the year: April to November

 Trail with yellow trail markers with a red circle

 Carry along a sufficient supply of water

Pervolàkia Gorge
On the wings of the wind

This exploration of Pervolàkia gorge concludes our array of the twenty most beautiful excursions on the island of Crete, the rough-hewn stones of a "komboloi," a rosary to be told bead by bead. At first glance, it has the same characteristics as the other nineteen gorges – all the morphological shadings of rock, vegetation and water, the European long-distance hiking trail, the botanical promenade - but the uniqueness of this excursion sets it quite apart.

The coastal road winds its way among hothouses, cane thickets and olive orchards from Ierapetra to Gouduras, on the extreme south-eastern point of the island near Kapsa monastery. A clearing of tamarisk trees and a small, rocky inlet in a curve of the road mark the beginning of Pervolàkia gorge. We recommend hiking up the gorge in order to avoid any anxiety that might be caused by sections of the trail which cross interminable, steep screes overlooking the

valley floor dotted with sharp pinnacles.

The white walls of the convent can be seen perched on a peak on the eastern edge of the canyon. The monastery dates back to the fifteenth century and over time the original nucleus was enlarged by the addition other buildings until it became a true religious community. Kapsa was abandoned after suffering repeated pirate forays, but it flourished once again thanks to Gerontogianni, a hermit from Crete who combined asceticism and organizational ability. Since then the monastery has been the destination of pilgrims who venerate the hermit like a saint.

It is mid-May, a clear day with a cobalt blue sky swept by a strong north-west wind that insinuates itself forcefully and implacably into the mountain rift. The leitmotif of this excursion is the wind, tyran-

nical and spiteful, and it forces us to proceed slowly. It subjugates us with its vehemence and toys with our caps until it manages to toss them into the chasm below. Each time the conformation of the rock face leads to a blind curve in the trail, the wind throws itself at us in fury, with the same effect as a door slamming shut during a storm.

At the entrance to the gorge a sign says "Farangi Pervolàkia" and "Kapsa," gives details about the three and a half kilometer-long trail and estimates that it will take over two hours to complete the hike. It gives us information about the rare fauna along the trail and lists fourteen different types of wildflowers. Unfortunately, the spring ended too soon this year and the blooming season was short. We are quickly surrounded by classical summer vegetation, oleanders, chastetree bushes, yellow asphodel with acid-green capsules, and aromatic shrubs like wild sage, summer savory, thyme and oregano.

There are th-
ee of us in our
mall group and
we get an ear-
y start along
the trail, which
nitially leads
pward along
the western
de of the gor-
e, winding its
way between
medium-sized
oulders. Later
n, in the more

ritical points, the trail is marked by an iron pole with a yellow squa-
e on top featuring a red circle. We immediately begin to climb, le-
ving behind the streambed which has become dry ahead of time,
nd we reach an open area among the crags of the gorge. On top
f a large stone we see a bird with light blue plumage streaked with
ark gray on the sides. It stares at us motionlessly for a moment,
hen flies away into the heart of the canyon. It is a monticola so-
tarius, or blue rock thrush, that has a preference for sunny rocks.
We are surrounded by an abundance of wild oregano, whose tiny
white inflorescence gives off its characteristic fragrance along the
ntire trail. Metamorphic rocks, dark limestone crossed or covered by

eruptive rocks, reddish crystal shale, conglomerates and yellow ma
color the sides of the ravine. The rocky walls are dotted with coun
tless immense, rocky cavities, open wounds that were created whe
blocks of the mountain detached themselves and crashed to the va
ley floor hundreds of thousands of years ago. After a quarter of a
hour the trail turns to the right along a ridge that was devastate
by a forest fire, leaving only sad, blackened stumps on the groun
We have been hiking for less that a kilometer when we enter a valle

full of pink oleanders an
come upon our first diff
culty: a series of boulder
that block our passage. W
"adventurously" clambe
over them with the hel
of a rudimental woode
ladder with seven rung
that is anchored to one c
the boulders. The hike al
ternates uphill and down
hill portions. Above, w
are immersed in a hars
mountain landscape an
enchanted by the line of the horizon which, behind us, reveals glim
pses of the glittering sea. Below, we are cheered by the presence c
small green oases with young plane trees and cane thickets, pro
tected by light green slabs of rock that have been smoothed by th
coursing water during the winter months. Halfway along the tra
the water that is still present at the bottom of a hollow forms a sma
waterfall, while the dry, sandy bottom of the hollow invites us t

ause for a moment. We have often taken breaks in these small are-
s that are protected by the rocky spurs. This one has a bright blue
gn that announces how many kilometers are still to be hiked in the
pposite direction from the one we have chosen, from the village of
ato Pervolàkia toward Kapsa monastery.

After two hours of hiking uphill, a wire fence that is broken in
any places and a light pole mark the end of the gorge. The landsca-
e flattens out into slopes that are cultivated with olive trees and
e first vegetable patches reappear.

The final portion of the trail, roughly five hundred meters, follows
dry riverbed that is cluttered with all kinds of garbage, worn-out
oes, rusty cans, plastic, sheep carcasses. Having left behind the
cky crags of the chasm, we sight the village of Kato Pervolàkia
sting in a broad valley, surrounded by cultivated hillsides that are
emmed in to the east by jagged peaks. A reinforced concrete bridge
ans the last part of the canyon and connects it to the village. The
titude - four hundred meters above sea level – encourages the
xuriant growth of thorny artichokes along the side of the road.
e small white houses that line the maze of narrow streets are em-
ellished with brightly colored geraniums growing in tin cans of all
zes that are lined up along the outside walls. Sweet peas poke up
etween the cobble stones. We enter the village café, a large, dark,
ctangular room decorated with a countertop, a refrigerator, two
bles and a couple of straw-bottomed chairs. There are few clients,
l very elderly. They are used to seeing excursionists, departing for
r arriving from the "farangi." They ask us where we come from,
azard a few words in Italian and then turn back to their game of
avli," the beloved Greek backgammon.

NEW
GUIDE

Alibertis Antonis

Follow us
In the GORGE of
SAMARIA

*A world of Nature, Life,
Legend and History*

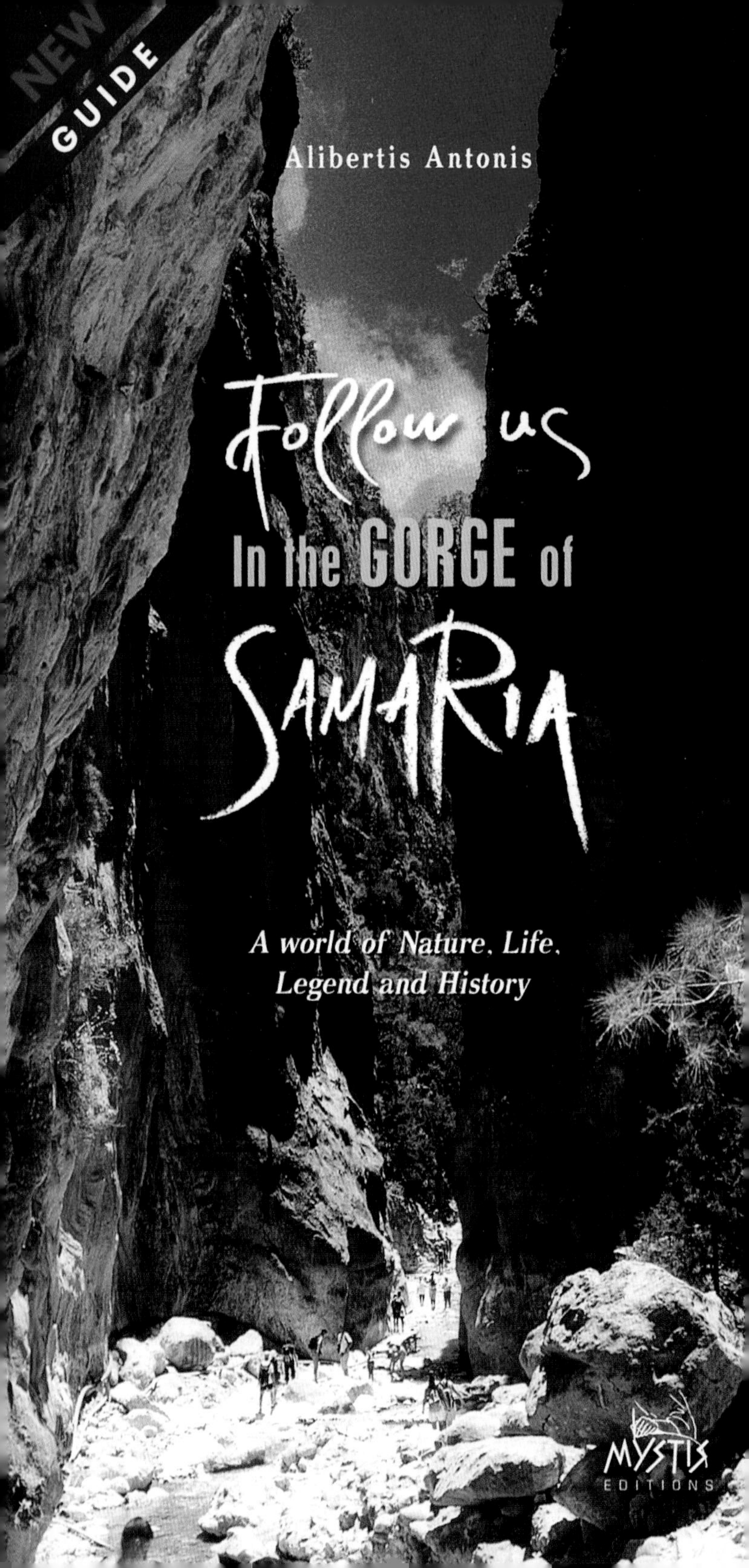

MYSTIS
EDITIONS

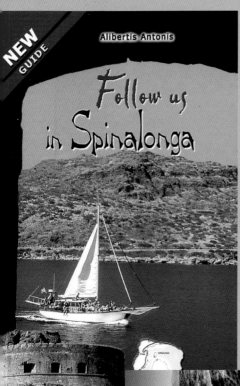

NEW GUIDE

Alibertis Antonis

Follow us in Spinalonga

...in the Venetian Castle, in the ottoman settlement.in the old city of lepers. The journey is incredible and the sea is seductive and mesmerizing.

ANDONIS VASILAKIS

CRETE

MYSTIS

Ant. Vasilakis

AGIA TRIADA
FESTOS
KOMMOS - MATALA

ADONIS S. VASILAKIS

THE GREAT INSCRIPTION
OF THE LAW CODE
of Gortyn

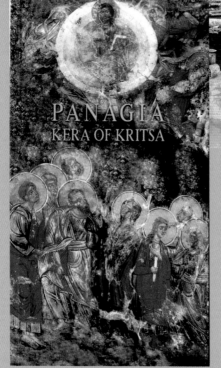

PANAGIA
KERA OF KRITSA

EDITIONS
MYSTIS
HERAKLION